THE COLLEGE VISIT JOURNAL:

CAMPUS VISITS DEMYSTIFIED

FIRST PAPERBACK EDITION JULY 2019

CONCEPTUALIZED & DESIGNED IN ATLANTA
ILLUSTRATIONS AND SOURCES LISTED ON OUR WEBSITE

ISBN 978-0-578-51805-3 (PAPERBACK)

PUBLISHING IMPRINT: MDM PUBLISHING

WWW.THECOLLEGEVISITJOURNAL.COM

THIS JOURNAL BELONGS TO:

_____

_____

_____

Applying to college is an exciting time. You're beginning to plan your future! It can also be a tedious process – with or without guidance. This journal was created to help you navigate a specific part of the process: the college campus visit.

I created this journal specifically for YOU to use as you visit various campuses in person or virtually. This journal will help you organize your thoughts and information and prompt you to think about how you'd like to spend the next four (yes, four!) years of your life.

Choosing a college is no small decision, so take it seriously.

In this journal, you will find enough space to evaluate 8 campuses with plenty of pages for notes. Before you start, flip through the entire first college visit section to get an idea of the format. Also, be sure to check out the resource pages in the back of the journal. You will find:

- Scholarship resources
- College ranking websites
- Sample text to use when communicating with campus personnel
- Key terms
- Financial aid resources

I can't wait to hear about the great things you are going to achieve!

Keep in touch,

Danielle

@TheCollegeVisitJournal

MANY THANKS

I couldn't have done this without the support of my family, friends and husband's 15+ years of college admission experience.

TABLE OF CONTENTS

A FRIENDLY REMINDER:

1. Ask Questions
2. Be Curious
3. You've Got This!

MY ACADEMIC PROFILE

This section is about you and your academic background.

You will complete it only once in this book, but update it as your class schedule, grades and test scores change.

It's a great reference when you meet with college counselors or if you meet with academic advisors who will help you decide which classes to take.

My High School:

_____

My Principal:

_____

My Counselor (name + best contact):

_____

ACADEMIC PROFILE	
GPA:	
SAT:	
ACT:	
Class Rank:	
# of AP Classes Taken:	
# of Honors Classes Taken:	
Earned College Credits: (if applicable)	

My Current Class Schedule:

_____   _____
_____   _____
_____   _____
_____   _____
_____   _____

WE'RE HERE!

CAMPUS VISIT #1

Fill in details about this college using the university's website and brochure or ask an admission counselor.

The next page contains basic facts about the school. Fill in the appropriate spaces and circle the words that best describe the college or university.

You will complete this page for each college campus visit.

DATE: 3/17/22

NAME OF COLLEGE / UNIVERSITY:

Providence College

LOCATION + CLOSEST BIG CITY:

Providence

NEAREST AIRPORT + MILES FROM HOME:

CAMPUS TYPE: *Circle one*

Rural I (Suburban) I Urban

SOCIAL MEDIA HANDLES:

MASCOT + SCHOOL COLORS:

Friars

STUDENT POPULATION:

4,000 +

MY DESIRED MAJOR / AREA OF INTEREST:

Business / History

INSTITUTION TYPE: *Circle one*

Public I (Private)

CATEGORY: *Circle one, if applicable*

Historically Black College & University (HBCU) I Men's

Tribal College I Women's I Military I 2-year

Hispanic Serving Institution (HSI) I (Religious Affiliation)

ACADEMIC CALENDAR: *Circle one*

(Semester) I Quarter I Trimester

CAMPUS VISIT #1

ON TOUR + CONTACTS

Take it all in and keep it organized using the checkboxes and prompts on the next few pages to evaluate your experience on campus.

Try to see as much as possible across campus and in the surrounding area and rate it on a scale from 1-5 (5 being the best) to get a good idea of the environment.

Plus, be sure to note the people you meet on campus and your peers on tour. Never underestimate the power of new connections!

If you need more space for notes, remember to use the notes pages at the end of this campus visit section!

I Visited...

☑ Student Center   ☑ Classroom   ☑ Newest Building

☑ Dining Hall   ☑ Rec Center/Gym   ☐ Local City Attractions

☑ Bookstore   ☐ Athletic Facilities   ☐ Health Center/Clinic

☑ Library   ☐ Dorms/Residence Halls   ☑ Study Spaces

☑ Academic Building   ☑ Alumni Center   ☑ Career Center

☐ Innovation Lab/Center   ☑ Oldest Building   ☐ Best Place to Take a Selfie

More On...

> Dorms / Residence Halls

☐ Suites / <u>Single Rooms</u> / <u>Shared</u>

☐ <u>Co-Ed</u> / All Male / All Female

☐ On-Campus Living Requirement: Yes / No

☐ Visitation Requirement / Curfew: <u>Yes</u> / No

☐ Laundry Fees: Yes / <u>No</u>

> Safety

☑ Keycard Access

☑ Visible Security / Blue Lights

☐ Safety App

☐ Self-Defense Training

☑ Parking Lots & Access

Now, Let's Rate... (On a scale of 1 to 5 - 5 being the best)

_2_ Overall Campus Beauty

_4_ Overall Campus Happiness

_2_ Greenery/Green space

_4_ Plans for Future Campus Growth

___ ADA Compliant/Accessible Areas*

___ Green Campus/Recycling Initiatives

___ Services (Disability, Health Center)

___ Weather

_4_ Traffic: Foot

___ Traffic: Vehicle

_3_ Noise Level

___ Campus Terrain

___ Tutoring/Math/Writing Center

_5_ My Tour Guide(s)

*Americans with Disabilities Act (ADA) ensures access to the built environment for people with disabilities. See the resources section for more information.

HOLD ON...

Take 30-60 seconds during the tour to quiet your mind and use your five senses to take in the space around you. What do you smell? Hear? Feel? Etc. If you want, close your eyes for better focus.

I'll wait.

My Tour Guide(s):

Name _____   Name _____
✉ Email _____   ✉ Email _____
@ Social Handles _____   @ Social Handles _____
🎓 Class of _____   🎓 Class of _____
📍 Hometown _____   📍 Hometown _____
🎓 Area of Study _____   🎓 Area of Study _____

My Admission Counselor:

👤 Name _____
✉ Email _____

Financial Aid Contact:

👤 Name _____
✉ Email _____

Students I Met + Want To Know Better:

Name _____   Name _____

Insta/Snap _____   Insta/Snap _____

Name _____   Name _____

Insta/Snap _____   Insta/Snap _____

Got business cards? Staple or paper clip them here:

CAMPUS VISIT #1

INFO SESSION

This section is helpful when you attend the info session. You will most likely learn about:

- Admission requirements, including test scores and important deadlines

- Campus-specific information such as history, on-campus activities and student support services

- Financial aid options and costs associated with attending the university

This may happen before or after the campus tour.

AVERAGES + RATES	
GPA	
SAT	
ACT	
Average Class Size	
Acceptance Rate *How many applicants were admitted?	
Retention Rate *The number of freshmen who returned in year two.	
Graduation Rate *How many students graduate in 6 years?	
Job Placement Rate	

NOTES + OTHER REQUIREMENTS

_____

_____

_____

_____

_____

_____

_____

_____

_____

_____

_____

_____

_____

_____

DEADLINES + THINGS TO KNOW	
Admission Deadlines	
Rolling Admission?	Yes I No
Regular	
Early Action (non-binding) *Students receive an early response to their application	
Early Decision (binding) *Requires student to enroll at admitted school. Generally, you can't withdraw application.	
Scholarship Deadlines	
Separate Scholarship Application Required?	Yes I No
Regular Deadline	
FAFSA Submission Deadlines	
FAFSA Priority Deadline *FAFSA opens October 1	
Date I submitted my FAFSA	

FINANCIAL AID

There are a number of ways to pay for college. The Free Application for Federal Student Aid (FAFSA) (studentaid.ed.gov/sa/fafsa) is required by most colleges and helps determine how much money your family can afford to pay for school.
To complete the form, you will need tax and income information from two years prior.

The FAFSA opens on October 1 and must be completed annually as long as you are enrolled in college.

Some schools may also require you to complete a CSS profile, which is used by some schools only for state and institutional aid (check the resources section for more information).

Let's take a look at the different types of aid:

> LOANS
Borrowed money for college; you must repay your loans, with interest

> GRANTS & SCHOLARSHIPS
Financial aid that doesn't have to be repaid (unless, for example, you withdraw from school and you will have to forfeit the money.)

> WORK-STUDY
A work program through which you earn money to help you pay for school.

(Source: https://studentaid.ed.gov)

TIP!
Ask your admission counselor about the requirements to be an RA (resident assistant)

OTHER WAYS TO PAY FOR COLLEGE:

1. **Tuition Reimbursement** – your current employer may help cover a portion or all of your education expenses.
2. **Part-time job** – ex. babysitting, server at local restaurant, tutoring at local school.
3. Take **Advanced Placement (AP)** classes in high school and test out of college courses.

EXPENSES

Cost of Attendance: $ _____

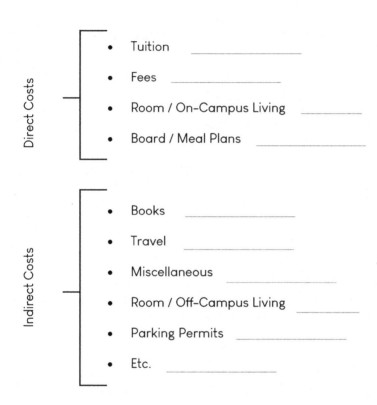

Direct Costs

- Tuition _____
- Fees _____
- Room / On-Campus Living _____
- Board / Meal Plans _____

Indirect Costs

- Books _____
- Travel _____
- Miscellaneous _____
- Room / Off-Campus Living _____
- Parking Permits _____
- Etc. _____

NOTES

_____

_____

_____

_____

CAMPUS VISIT #1

THE ASSESSMENT

The gauges on the next page measure engagement.

Draw an arrow to express how empty or full you feel in regards to each category during the information session and campus tour. For example, during moments of enthusiasm or delight and intense concentration, you may feel more engaged, present in the moment, or full.

Three categories are provided for you, but use the two blank ones to create your own measurements of fullness. Here's an example:

Then, use the notes space to reflect on your feelings in each category.

ENGAGED DELIVERY OF INFORMATION FACILITIES/SPACE

Notes

_____

_____

_____

_____

_____

_____

CAMPUS VISIT #1

LET'S TALK PEOPLE

Use the space on the next page to reflect on the people you meet and see across campus during your tour.

Take notes about your thoughts.

I was impressed by:

_____

_____

I had concerns about:

_____

_____

I'd like more time to talk to:
Use the writing samples in the resource section for pointers!

_____

_____

I'd like to learn more about:
(Majors, Internships, Work-Study Opportunities, Overnight Experiences, etc.)

_____

_____

Professors I met:

_____

_____

Administrators I met:

_____

_____

Overall, students on campus seem to be:

_____

Notable / famous alumni:

_____

_____

Alumni I may know (family, friends, former classmates, etc.):

_____

_____

Today I learned:

_____

_____

⚡

CHALLENGE: STEP OUT OF YOUR COMFORT ZONE!

Break the ice with people you meet by asking questions like these. Use the notes pages to jot down their answers!

> What was your greatest challenge in school? It could be related to academics, social, extracurricular, career, etc.

> If you could study abroad anywhere in the world, where would it be?

> Who would you like to trade places with for a week?

> What will you miss most about high school?

> What are you most looking forward to in college?

> How do you define integrity?

> What's your biggest accomplishment?

> If time and money weren't an issue, what kind of business would you have?

BET ON YOURSELF AND BE... MORE THAN

- MAVERICK CARTER, BUSINESS ENTREPRENEUR

COMMENCEMENT SPEAKER – 2019
UNIVERSITY OF SOUTHERN CALIFORNIA
ANNENBERG SCHOOL FOR COMMUNICATION AND JOURNALISM

CAMPUS VISIT #1

PERSONAL REFLECTION

Complete this section AFTER your campus visit.

Consider your personality, characteristics, talents, must-haves and goals when completing the questions and scales on the next page as it relates to this college campus visit.

Name of college:

_____

Why am I considering this college?

_____

What really interests me (academic and extracurricular) that's offered here?

_____

How would I describe the campus diversity?

_____

Knowing my must-haves and nice-to-haves, how does this college measure up?

_____

• • • • • • • • • • • •

Using the scale below, indicate your level of agreement for each "fit" category.

This campus is a realistic...	Strongly Disagree	Disagree	Neither Agree nor Disagree	Agree	Strongly Agree
Academic Fit:	◯	◯	◯	◯	◯
Diversity Fit:	◯	◯	◯	◯	◯
Social Fit:	◯	◯	◯	◯	◯
Financial Fit:	◯	◯	◯	◯	◯
Athletic Fit:	◯	◯	◯	◯	◯
Overall Fit:	◯	◯	◯	◯	◯

• • • • • • • • • • • •

Next steps for this school:

☐ Start Application   ☐ Submit Mid-Year Transcripts   ☐ Alumni Interview

☐ Thank You Note   ☐ Request More Information   ☐ Pay App Fee

☐ Finish Application   ☐ Submit FAFSA   ☐ Pay Deposit

☐ Other:

CAMPUS VISIT #1

STATUS & PROGRESS

Use the status circles to track your progress for each application deliverable for this university. Once the deliverable is complete, write the completion date in the "100%" circle.

Name of College _____

APPLICATION ○ ○ ○ ○ ○ ○ ○ ○ ○ ○ ○
10%   50%   100% N/A

ESSAY ○ ○ ○ ○ ○ ○ ○ ○ ○ ○ ○
10%   50%   100% N/A

TEST SCORE
SUBMISSIONS ○ ○ ○ ○ ○ ○ ○ ○ ○ ○ ○
10%   50%   100% N/A

TEACHER RECS ○ ○ ○ ○ ○ ○ ○ ○ ○ ○ ○
10%   50%   100% N/A

COUNSELOR
RECS ○ ○ ○ ○ ○ ○ ○ ○ ○ ○ ○
10%   50%   100% N/A

SUPPLEMENT/
EXPRESSION PAGE ○ ○ ○ ○ ○ ○ ○ ○ ○ ○ ○
10%   50%   100% N/A

FAFSA ○ ○ ○ ○ ○ ○ ○ ○ ○ ○ ○
10%   50%   100% N/A

SCHOLARSHIP
APP #1 ○ ○ ○ ○ ○ ○ ○ ○ ○ ○ ○
10%   50%   100% N/A

SCHOLARSHIP
APP #2 ○ ○ ○ ○ ○ ○ ○ ○ ○ ○ ○
10%   50%   100% N/A

_____ ○ ○ ○ ○ ○ ○ ○ ○ ○ ○ ○
10%   50%   100% N/A

BIG IDEAS & RANDOM THOUGHTS

These are bullet pages. Use them as you wish - for notes, to-do lists, to sketch, draw or schedule tasks. Let your imagination drive you.

I'm Curious...

How would your best friend describe you? Include your strengths!

BIG IDEA!
Send this description to your guidance counselor so s/he can use it when writing your letter of recommendation.

NOTES

Pros:	Cons:
Vibrant community	Bad architecture
Many social/nightlife opportunities	Only seniors can live off campus
Good study abroad program	

NOTES

YOU'VE GOT THIS!

CAMPUS VISIT #2

Fill in details about this college using the university's website and brochure or ask an admission counselor.

The next page contains basic facts about the school. Fill in the appropriate spaces and circle the words that best describe the college or university.

You will complete this page for each college campus visit.

NAME OF COLLEGE / UNIVERSITY:

Connecticut College

LOCATION + CLOSEST BIG CITY:

New London

NEAREST AIRPORT + MILES FROM HOME:

CAMPUS TYPE: *Circle one*

Rural | <u>Suburban</u> | Urban

SOCIAL MEDIA HANDLES:

MASCOT + SCHOOL COLORS:

Camel

STUDENT POPULATION:

1,800

MY DESIRED MAJOR / AREA OF INTEREST:

INSTITUTION TYPE: *Circle one*

Public | <u>Private</u>

CATEGORY: *Circle one, if applicable*

Historically Black College & University (HBCU) | Men's

Tribal College | Women's | Military | 2-year

Hispanic Serving Institution (HSI) | Religious Affiliation

ACADEMIC CALENDAR: *Circle one*

Semester | Quarter | Trimester

CAMPUS VISIT #2

ON TOUR + CONTACTS

Take it all in and keep it organized using the checkboxes and prompts on the next few pages to evaluate your experience on campus.

Try to see as much as possible across campus and in the surrounding area and rate it on a scale from 1-5 (5 being the best) to get a good idea of the environment.

Plus, be sure to note the people you meet on campus and your peers on tour. Never underestimate the power of new connections!

If you need more space for notes, remember to use the notes pages at the end of this campus visit section!

I Visited...

- ☑ Student Center
- ☑ Dining Hall
- ☐ Bookstore
- ☑ Library
- ☑ Academic Building
- ☐ Innovation Lab/Center

- ☐ Classroom
- ☐ Rec Center/Gym
- ☐ Athletic Facilities
- ☑ Dorms/Residence Halls
- ☐ Alumni Center
- ☐ Oldest Building

- ☐ Newest Building
- ☐ Local City Attractions
- ☐ Health Center/Clinic
- ☐ Study Spaces
- ☑ Career Center
- ☐ Best Place to Take a Selfie

More On...

> Dorms / Residence Halls

- ☐ Suites / Single Rooms / Shared
- ☐ Co-Ed / All Male / All Female
- ☐ On-Campus Living Requirement: Yes / No
- ☐ Visitation Requirement / Curfew: Yes / No
- ☐ Laundry Fees: Yes / No

> Safety

- ☑ Keycard Access
- ☐ Visible Security / Blue Lights
- ☐ Safety App
- ☐ Self-Defense Training
- ☐ Parking Lots & Access

Now, Let's Rate... (On a scale of 1 to 5 - 5 being the best)

- __4__ Overall Campus Beauty
- __3__ Overall Campus Happiness
- __5__ Greenery/Green space
- _____ Plans for Future Campus Growth
- _____ ADA Compliant/Accessible Areas*
- _____ Green Campus/Recycling Initiatives
- _____ Services (Disability, Health Center)

- _____ Weather
- _____ Traffic: Foot
- _____ Traffic: Vehicle
- _____ Noise Level
- _____ Campus Terrain
- _____ Tutoring/Math/Writing Center
- __3__ My Tour Guide(s)

*Americans with Disabilities Act (ADA) ensures access to the built environment for people with disabilities. See the resources section for more information.

HOLD ON...

Take 30-60 seconds during the tour to quiet your mind and use your five senses to take in the space around you. What do you smell? Hear? Feel? Etc. If you want, close your eyes for better focus.

I'll wait.

My Tour Guide(s):

Name _____   Name _____

✉ Email _____   ✉ Email _____

@ Social Handles _____   @ Social Handles _____

🎓 Class of _____   🎓 Class of _____

📍 Hometown _____   📍 Hometown _____

🏫 Area of Study _____   🏫 Area of Study _____

My Admission Counselor:

👤 Name _____

✉ Email _____

Financial Aid Contact:

👤 Name _____

✉ Email _____

Students I Met + Want To Know Better:

Name _____   Name _____

Insta/Snap _____   Insta/Snap _____

Name _____   Name _____

Insta/Snap _____   Insta/Snap _____

Got business cards? Staple or paper clip them here:

CAMPUS VISIT #2

INFO SESSION

This section is helpful when you attend the info session. You will most likely learn about:

- Admission requirements, including test scores and important deadlines

- Campus-specific information such as history, on-campus activities and student support services

- Financial aid options and costs associated with attending the university

This may happen before or after the campus tour.

AVERAGES + RATES	
GPA	
SAT	
ACT	
Average Class Size	
Acceptance Rate *How many applicants were admitted?*	
Retention Rate *The number of freshmen who returned in year two.*	
Graduation Rate *How many students graduate in 6 years?*	
Job Placement Rate	

NOTES + OTHER REQUIREMENTS

_____

_____

_____

_____

_____

_____

_____

_____

_____

_____

_____

_____

_____

_____

_____

_____

DEADLINES + THINGS TO KNOW	
Admission Deadlines	
Rolling Admission?	Yes | No
Regular	
Early Action (non-binding) *Students receive an early response to their application*	
Early Decision (binding) *Requires student to enroll at admitted school. Generally, you can't withdraw application.*	
Scholarship Deadlines	
Separate Scholarship Application Required?	Yes | No
Regular Deadline	
FAFSA Submission Deadlines	
FAFSA Priority Deadline *FAFSA opens October 1*	
Date I submitted my FAFSA	

FINANCIAL AID

There are a number of ways to pay for college. The Free Application for Federal Student Aid (FAFSA) (studentaid.ed.gov/sa/fafsa) is required by most colleges and helps determine how much money your family can afford to pay for school.
To complete the form, you will need tax and income information from two years prior.

The FAFSA opens on October 1 and must be completed annually as long as you are enrolled in college.

Some schools may also require you to complete a CSS profile, which is used by some schools only for state and institutional aid (check the resources section for more information).

Let's take a look at the different types of aid:

> LOANS

Borrowed money for college, you must repay your loans, with interest.

> GRANTS & SCHOLARSHIPS

Financial aid that doesn't have to be repaid (unless, for example, you withdraw from school and you will have to forfeit the money.)

> WORK-STUDY

A work program through which you earn money to help you pay for school.

(Source: https://studentaid.ed.gov)

TIP!
Ask your admission counselor about the requirements to be an RA (resident assistant)

OTHER WAYS TO PAY FOR COLLEGE:

1. **Tuition Reimbursement** – your current employer may help cover a portion or all of your education expenses.

2. **Part-time job** – ex. babysitting, server at local restaurant, tutoring at local school.

3. Take **Advanced Placement (AP)** classes in high school and test out of college courses.

EXPENSES

Cost of Attendance: $ _____

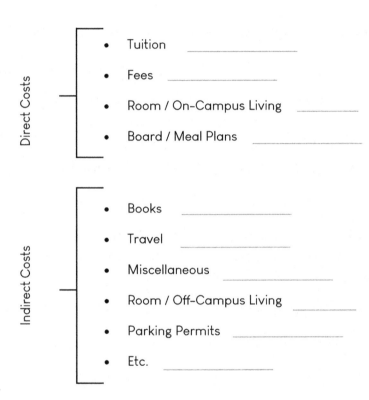

Direct Costs

- Tuition _____
- Fees _____
- Room / On-Campus Living _____
- Board / Meal Plans _____

Indirect Costs

- Books _____
- Travel _____
- Miscellaneous _____
- Room / Off-Campus Living _____
- Parking Permits _____
- Etc. _____

NOTES

_____

_____

_____

_____

CAMPUS VISIT #2

THE ASSESSMENT

The gauges on the next page measure engagement.

Draw an arrow to express how empty or full you feel in regards to each category during the information session and campus tour. For example, during moments of enthusiasm or delight and intense concentration, you may feel more engaged, present in the moment, or full.

Three categories are provided for you, but use the two blank ones to create your own measurements of fullness. Here's an example:

Then, use the notes space to reflect on your feelings in each category.

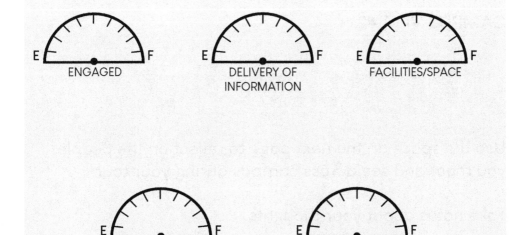

ENGAGED

DELIVERY OF
INFORMATION

FACILITIES/SPACE

Notes

_____

_____

_____

_____

_____

CAMPUS VISIT #2

LET'S TALK PEOPLE

Use the space on the next page to reflect on the people you meet and see across campus during your tour.

Take notes about your thoughts.

I was impressed by:

_____

_____

I had concerns about:

_____

_____

I'd like more time to talk to:
Use the writing samples in the resource section for pointers!

_____

_____

I'd like to learn more about:
(Majors, Internships, Work-Study Opportunities, Overnight Experiences, etc.)

_____

_____

Professors I met:

_____

_____

Administrators I met:

_____

_____

Overall, students on campus seem to be:

_____

Notable / famous alumni:

_____

_____

Alumni I may know (family, friends, former classmates, etc.):

_____

_____

Today I learned:

_____

_____

⚡

CHALLENGE: STEP OUT OF YOUR COMFORT ZONE!

Break the ice with people you meet by asking questions like these. Use the notes pages to jot down their answers!

> What was your greatest challenge in school? It could be related to academics, social, extracurricular, career, etc.

> If you could study abroad anywhere in the world, where would it be?

> Who would you like to trade places with for a week?

> What will you miss most about high school?

> What are you most looking forward to in college?

> How do you define integrity?

> What's your biggest accomplishment?

> If time and money weren't an issue, what kind of business would you have?

THERE IS NO INNOVATION AND CREATIVITY WITHOUT FAILURE.

PERIOD.

- DR. BRENE' BROWN
AUTHOR + RESEARCH PROFESSOR, UNIVERSITY OF HOUSTON

THE CALL TO COURAGE
NETFLIX SPECIAL, 2019

CAMPUS VISIT #2

PERSONAL REFLECTION

Complete this section AFTER your campus visit.

Consider your personality, characteristics, talents, must-haves and goals when completing the questions and scales on the next page as it relates to this college campus visit.

Name of college:

Why am I considering this college?

What really interests me (academic and extracurricular) that's offered here?

How would I describe the campus diversity?

Knowing my must-haves and nice-to-haves, how does this college measure up?

· · · · · · · · · · · · ·

Using the scale below, indicate your level of agreement for each "fit" category.

This campus is a realistic...	Strongly Disagree	Disagree	Neither Agree nor Disagree	Agree	Strongly Agree
Academic Fit:	◯	◯	◯	◯	◯
Diversity Fit:	◯	◯	◯	◯	◯
Social Fit:	◯	◯	◯	◯	◯
Financial Fit:	◯	◯	◯	◯	◯
Athletic Fit:	◯	◯	◯	◯	◯
Overall Fit:	◯	◯	◯	◯	◯

· · · · · · · · · · · · ·

Next steps for this school:

☐ Start Application ☐ Submit Mid-Year Transcripts ☐ Alumni Interview

☐ Thank You Note ☐ Request More Information ☐ Pay App Fee

☐ Finish Application ☐ Submit FAFSA ☐ Pay Deposit

☐ Other:

CAMPUS VISIT #2

STATUS & PROGRESS

Use the status circles to track your progress for each application deliverable for this university. Once the deliverable is complete, write the completion date in the "100%" circle.

Name of College _____

APPLICATION ○ ○ ○ ○ ○ ○ ○ ○ ○ ○ ○
10%   50%   100% N/A

ESSAY ○ ○ ○ ○ ○ ○ ○ ○ ○ ○ ○
10%   50%   100% N/A

TEST SCORE
SUBMISSIONS ○ ○ ○ ○ ○ ○ ○ ○ ○ ○ ○
10%   50%   100% N/A

TEACHER RECS ○ ○ ○ ○ ○ ○ ○ ○ ○ ○ ○
10%   50%   100% N/A

COUNSELOR
RECS ○ ○ ○ ○ ○ ○ ○ ○ ○ ○ ○
10%   50%   100% N/A

SUPPLEMENT/
EXPRESSION PAGE ○ ○ ○ ○ ○ ○ ○ ○ ○ ○ ○
10%   50%   100% N/A

FAFSA ○ ○ ○ ○ ○ ○ ○ ○ ○ ○ ○
10%   50%   100% N/A

SCHOLARSHIP
APP #1 ○ ○ ○ ○ ○ ○ ○ ○ ○ ○ ○
10%   50%   100% N/A

SCHOLARSHIP
APP #2 ○ ○ ○ ○ ○ ○ ○ ○ ○ ○ ○
10%   50%   100% N/A

_____ ○ ○ ○ ○ ○ ○ ○ ○ ○ ○ ○
10%   50%   100% N/A

BIG IDEAS & RANDOM THOUGHTS

These are bullet pages. Use them as you wish - for notes, to-do lists, to sketch, draw or schedule tasks. Let your imagination drive you.

I'm Curious...

Have you ever volunteered? If so, what attracted you to the opportunity and what did you learn from it?

BIG IDEA!
Send this description to your guidance counselor so s/he can use it when writing your letter of recommendation.

NOTES

Wondering about social life, I have
a feeling cliques are formed

NOTES

STAY HYDRATED...

CAMPUS VISIT #3

Fill in details about this college using the university's website and brochure or ask an admission counselor.

The next page contains basic facts about the school. Fill in the appropriate spaces and circle the words that best describe the college or university.

You will complete this page for each college campus visit.

DATE: ___ / ___ / ___

NAME OF COLLEGE / UNIVERSITY:

_____

 LOCATION + CLOSEST BIG CITY:

_____

NEAREST AIRPORT + MILES FROM HOME:

_____

CAMPUS TYPE: *Circle one*

Rural | Suburban | Urban

 SOCIAL MEDIA HANDLES:

_____

 MASCOT + SCHOOL COLORS:

_____

 STUDENT POPULATION:

_____

 MY DESIRED MAJOR / AREA OF INTEREST:

_____

 INSTITUTION TYPE: *Circle one*

Public | Private

CATEGORY: *Circle one, if applicable*

Historically Black College & University (HBCU) | Men's

Tribal College | Women's | Military | 2-year

Hispanic Serving Institution (HSI) | Religious Affiliation

 ACADEMIC CALENDAR: *Circle one*

Semester | Quarter | Trimester

CAMPUS VISIT #3

ON TOUR + CONTACTS

Take it all in and keep it organized using the checkboxes and prompts on the next few pages to evaluate your experience on campus.

Try to see as much as possible across campus and in the surrounding area and rate it on a scale from 1-5 (5 being the best) to get a good idea of the environment.

Plus, be sure to note the people you meet on campus and your peers on tour. Never underestimate the power of new connections!

If you need more space for notes, remember to use the notes pages at the end of this campus visit section!

I Visited...

☐ Student Center   ☐ Classroom   ☐ Newest Building

☐ Dining Hall   ☐ Rec Center/Gym   ☐ Local City Attractions

☐ Bookstore   ☐ Athletic Facilities   ☐ Health Center/Clinic

☐ Library   ☐ Dorms/Residence Halls   ☐ Study Spaces

☐ Academic Building   ☐ Alumni Center   ☐ Career Center

☐ Innovation Lab/Center   ☐ Oldest Building   ☐ Best Place to Take a Selfie

More On...

> Dorms / Residence Halls

☐ Suites / Single Rooms / Shared

☐ Co-Ed / All Male / All Female

☐ On-Campus Living Requirement: Yes / No

☐ Visitation Requirement / Curfew: Yes / No

☐ Laundry Fees: Yes / No

> Safety

☐ Keycard Access

☐ Visible Security / Blue Lights

☐ Safety App

☐ Self-Defense Training

☐ Parking Lots & Access

Now, Let's Rate... (On a scale of 1 to 5 - 5 being the best)

_____ Overall Campus Beauty

_____ Overall Campus Happiness

_____ Greenery/Green space

_____ Plans for Future Campus Growth

_____ ADA Compliant/Accessible Areas*

_____ Green Campus/Recycling Initiatives

_____ Services (Disability, Health Center)

_____ Weather

_____ Traffic: Foot

_____ Traffic: Vehicle

_____ Noise Level

_____ Campus Terrain

_____ Tutoring/Math/Writing Center

_____ My Tour Guide(s)

*Americans with Disabilities Act (ADA) ensures access to the built environment for people with disabilities. See the resources section for more information.

HOLD ON...

Take 30-60 seconds during the tour to quiet your mind and use your five senses to take in the space around you. What do you smell? Hear? Feel? Etc. If you want, close your eyes for better focus.

I'll wait.

My Tour Guide(s):

Name _____   Name _____

✉ Email _____   ✉ Email _____

@ Social Handles _____   @ Social Handles _____

🎓 Class of _____   🎓 Class of _____

◉ Hometown _____   ◉ Hometown _____

🏫 Area of Study _____   🏫 Area of Study _____

My Admission Counselor:

👤 Name _____

✉ Email _____

Financial Aid Contact:

👤 Name _____

✉ Email _____

Students I Met + Want To Know Better:

Name _____   Name _____

Insta/Snap _____   Insta/Snap _____

Name _____   Name _____

Insta/Snap _____   Insta/Snap _____

Got business cards? Staple or paper clip them here:

CAMPUS VISIT #3

INFO SESSION

This section is helpful when you attend the info session. You will most likely learn about:

- Admission requirements, including test scores and important deadlines

- Campus-specific information such as history, on-campus activities and student support services

- Financial aid options and costs associated with attending the university

This may happen before or after the campus tour.

AVERAGES + RATES	
GPA	
SAT	
ACT	
Average Class Size	
Acceptance Rate *How many applicants were admitted?*	
Retention Rate *The number of freshmen who returned in year two.*	
Graduation Rate *How many students graduate in 6 years?*	
Job Placement Rate	

NOTES + OTHER REQUIREMENTS

_____

_____

_____

_____

_____

_____

_____

_____

_____

_____

_____

_____

_____

_____

DEADLINES + THINGS TO KNOW	
Admission Deadlines	
Rolling Admission?	Yes | No
Regular	
Early Action (non-binding) *Students receive an early response to their application*	
Early Decision (binding) *Requires student to enroll at admitted school. Generally, you can't withdraw application.*	
Scholarship Deadlines	
Separate Scholarship Application Required?	Yes | No
Regular Deadline	
FAFSA Submission Deadlines	
FAFSA Priority Deadline *FAFSA opens October 1*	
Date I submitted my FAFSA	

FINANCIAL AID

There are a number of ways to pay for college. The Free Application for Federal Student Aid (FAFSA) (studentaid.ed.gov/sa/fafsa) is required by most colleges and helps determine how much money your family can afford to pay for school.
To complete the form, you will need tax and income information from two years prior.

The FAFSA opens on October 1 and must be completed annually as long as you are enrolled in college.

Some schools may also require you to complete a CSS profile, which is used by some schools only for state and institutional aid (check the resources section for more information).

Let's take a look at the different types of aid:

> LOANS
Borrowed money for college; you must repay your loans with interest.

> GRANTS & SCHOLARSHIPS
Financial aid that doesn't have to be repaid (unless, for example, you withdraw from school and you will have to forfeit the money.)

> WORK-STUDY
A work program through which you earn money to help you pay for school.

(Source: https://studentaid.ed.gov)

TIP!
Ask your admission counselor about the requirements to be an RA (resident assistant)

OTHER WAYS TO PAY FOR COLLEGE:

1. **Tuition Reimbursement** – your current employer may help cover a portion or all of your education expenses.

2. **Part-time job** - ex. babysitting, server at local restaurant, tutoring at local school.

3. Take **Advanced Placement (AP)** classes in high school and test out of college courses.

EXPENSES

Cost of Attendance: $ _____

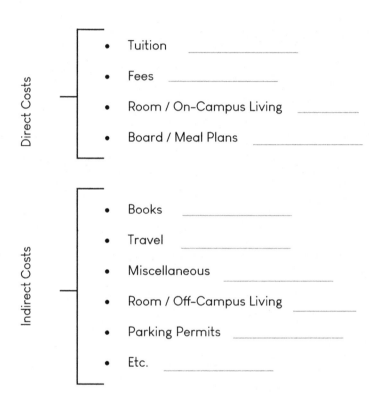

Direct Costs

- Tuition _____
- Fees _____
- Room / On-Campus Living _____
- Board / Meal Plans _____

Indirect Costs

- Books _____
- Travel _____
- Miscellaneous _____
- Room / Off-Campus Living _____
- Parking Permits _____
- Etc. _____

NOTES

_____

_____

_____

_____

THE ASSESSMENT

The gauges on the next page measure engagement.

Draw an arrow to express how empty or full you feel in regards to each category during the information session and campus tour. For example, during moments of enthusiasm or delight and intense concentration, you may feel more engaged, present in the moment, or full.

Three categories are provided for you, but use the two blank ones to create your own measurements of fullness. Here's an example:

Then, use the notes space to reflect on your feelings in each category.

ENGAGED

DELIVERY OF INFORMATION

FACILITIES/SPACE

Notes

_____

_____

_____

_____

_____

CAMPUS VISIT #3

LET'S TALK PEOPLE

Use the space on the next page to reflect on the people you meet and see across campus during your tour.

Take notes about your thoughts.

I was impressed by:

_____

_____

I had concerns about:

_____

_____

I'd like more time to talk to:
Use the writing samples in the resource section for pointers!

_____

_____

I'd like to learn more about:
(Majors, Internships, Work-Study Opportunities, Overnight Experiences, etc.)

_____

_____

Professors I met:

_____

_____

Administrators I met:

_____

_____

Overall, students on campus seem to be:

_____

Notable / famous alumni:

_____

_____

Alumni I may know (family, friends, former classmates, etc.):

_____

_____

Today I learned:

_____

_____

⚡ CHALLENGE: STEP OUT OF YOUR COMFORT ZONE!

Break the ice with people you meet by asking questions like these. Use the notes pages to jot down their answers!

> What was your greatest challenge in school? It could be related to academics, social, extracurricular, career, etc.

> If you could study abroad anywhere in the world, where would it be?

> Who would you like to trade places with for a week?

> What will you miss most about high school?

> What are you most looking forward to in college?

> How do you define integrity?

> What's your biggest accomplishment?

> If time and money weren't an issue, what kind of business would you have?

NEVER LET FAILURE PARALYZE YOU.

FAILURE ISN'T FATAL.

- DR. NICOLE COSBY
PROFESSOR + ATHLETIC TRAINING PROGRAM
DIRECTOR, POINT LOMA NAZARENE UNIVERSITY

COMMENCEMENT SPEAKER - 2019
POINT LOMA NAZARENE UNIVERSITY

CAMPUS VISIT #3

PERSONAL REFLECTION

Complete this section AFTER your campus visit.

Consider your personality, characteristics, talents, must-haves and goals when completing the questions and scales on the next page as it relates to this college campus visit.

Name of college:

Why am I considering this college?

What really interests me (academic and extracurricular) that's offered here?

How would I describe the campus diversity?

Knowing my must-haves and nice-to-haves, how does this college measure up?

· · · · · · · · · · · · ·

Using the scale below, indicate your level of agreement for each "fit" category.

This campus is a realistic...	Strongly Disagree	Disagree	Neither Agree nor Disagree	Agree	Strongly Agree
Academic Fit:	○	○	○	○	○
Diversity Fit:	○	○	○	○	○
Social Fit:	○	○	○	○	○
Financial Fit:	○	○	○	○	○
Athletic Fit:	○	○	○	○	○
Overall Fit:	○	○	○	○	○

· · · · · · · · · · · · ·

Next steps for this school:

☐ Start Application ☐ Submit Mid-Year Transcripts ☐ Alumni Interview

☐ Thank You Note ☐ Request More Information ☐ Pay App Fee

☐ Finish Application ☐ Submit FAFSA ☐ Pay Deposit

☐ Other:

CAMPUS VISIT #3

STATUS & PROGRESS

Use the status circles to track your progress for each application deliverable for this university. Once the deliverable is complete, write the completion date in the "100%" circle.

Name of College _____

APPLICATION ○ ○ ○ ○ ○ ○ ○ ○ ○ ○ ○
　　　　　　 10%　　　　50%　　　　100%　N/A

ESSAY ○ ○ ○ ○ ○ ○ ○ ○ ○ ○ ○
　　　　10%　　　　50%　　　　100%　N/A

TEST SCORE
SUBMISSIONS ○ ○ ○ ○ ○ ○ ○ ○ ○ ○ ○
　　　　　　 10%　　　　50%　　　　100%　N/A

TEACHER RECS ○ ○ ○ ○ ○ ○ ○ ○ ○ ○ ○
　　　　　　　10%　　　　50%　　　　100%　N/A

COUNSELOR
RECS ○ ○ ○ ○ ○ ○ ○ ○ ○ ○ ○
　　　 10%　　　　50%　　　　100%　N/A

SUPPLEMENT/
EXPRESSION PAGE ○ ○ ○ ○ ○ ○ ○ ○ ○ ○ ○
　　　　　　　　 10%　　　　50%　　　　100%　N/A

FAFSA ○ ○ ○ ○ ○ ○ ○ ○ ○ ○ ○
　　　　10%　　　　50%　　　　100%　N/A

SCHOLARSHIP
APP #1 ○ ○ ○ ○ ○ ○ ○ ○ ○ ○ ○
　　　　10%　　　　50%　　　　100%　N/A

SCHOLARSHIP
APP #2 ○ ○ ○ ○ ○ ○ ○ ○ ○ ○ ○
　　　　10%　　　　50%　　　　100%　N/A

_____ ○ ○ ○ ○ ○ ○ ○ ○ ○ ○ ○
　　　　　　　　 10%　　　　50%　　　　100%　N/A

BIG IDEAS & RANDOM THOUGHTS

These are bullet pages. Use them as you wish - for notes, to-do lists, to sketch, draw or schedule tasks. Let your imagination drive you.

I'm Curious...

What do you think is the best invention currently? How would you improve upon it?

NOTES

NOTES

YOU'RE UNIQUELY YOU. DON'T FORGET IT!

CAMPUS VISIT #4

Fill in details about this college using the university's website and brochure or ask an admission counselor.

The next page contains basic facts about the school. Fill in the appropriate spaces and circle the words that best describe the college or university.

You will complete this page for each college campus visit.

NAME OF COLLEGE / UNIVERSITY:

LOCATION + CLOSEST BIG CITY:

NEAREST AIRPORT + MILES FROM HOME:

CAMPUS TYPE: *Circle one*

Rural I Suburban I Urban

SOCIAL MEDIA HANDLES:

MASCOT + SCHOOL COLORS:

STUDENT POPULATION:

MY DESIRED MAJOR / AREA OF INTEREST:

INSTITUTION TYPE: *Circle one*

Public I Private

CATEGORY: *Circle one, if applicable*

Historically Black College & University (HBCU) I Men's

Tribal College I Women's I Military I 2-year

Hispanic Serving Institution (HSI) I Religious Affiliation

ACADEMIC CALENDAR: *Circle one*

Semester I Quarter I Trimester

CAMPUS VISIT #4

ON TOUR + CONTACTS

Take it all in and keep it organized using the checkboxes and prompts on the next few pages to evaluate your experience on campus.

Try to see as much as possible across campus and in the surrounding area and rate it on a scale from 1-5 (5 being the best) to get a good idea of the environment.

Plus, be sure to note the people you meet on campus and your peers on tour. Never underestimate the power of new connections!

If you need more space for notes, remember to use the notes pages at the end of this campus visit section!

I Visited...

- [ ] Student Center
- [ ] Dining Hall
- [ ] Bookstore
- [ ] Library
- [ ] Academic Building
- [ ] Innovation Lab/Center
- [ ] Classroom
- [ ] Rec Center/Gym
- [ ] Athletic Facilities
- [ ] Dorms/Residence Halls
- [ ] Alumni Center
- [ ] Oldest Building
- [ ] Newest Building
- [ ] Local City Attractions
- [ ] Health Center/Clinic
- [ ] Study Spaces
- [ ] Career Center
- [ ] Best Place to Take a Selfie

More On...

> Dorms / Residence Halls

- [ ] Suites / Single Rooms / Shared
- [ ] Co-Ed / All Male / All Female
- [ ] On-Campus Living Requirement: Yes / No
- [ ] Visitation Requirement / Curfew: Yes / No
- [ ] Laundry Fees: Yes / No

> Safety

- [ ] Keycard Access
- [ ] Visible Security / Blue Lights
- [ ] Safety App
- [ ] Self-Defense Training
- [ ] Parking Lots & Access

Now, Let's Rate... (On a scale of 1 to 5 - 5 being the best)

_____ Overall Campus Beauty

_____ Overall Campus Happiness

_____ Greenery/Green space

_____ Plans for Future Campus Growth

_____ ADA Compliant/Accessible Areas*

_____ Green Campus/Recycling Initiatives

_____ Services (Disability, Health Center)

_____ Weather

_____ Traffic: Foot

_____ Traffic: Vehicle

_____ Noise Level

_____ Campus Terrain

_____ Tutoring/Math/Writing Center

_____ My Tour Guide(s)

*Americans with Disabilities Act (ADA) ensures access to the built environment for people with disabilities. See the resources section for more information.

HOLD ON...

Take 30-60 seconds during the tour to quiet your mind and use your five senses to take in the space around you. What do you smell? Hear? Feel? Etc. If you want, close your eyes for better focus.

I'll wait.

My Tour Guide(s):

Name _____

✉ Email _____

@ Social Handles _____

🎓 Class of _____

📍 Hometown _____

🏫 Area of Study _____

Name _____

✉ Email _____

@ Social Handles _____

🎓 Class of _____

📍 Hometown _____

🏫 Area of Study _____

My Admission Counselor:

👤 Name _____

✉ Email _____

Financial Aid Contact:

👤 Name _____

✉ Email _____

Students I Met + Want To Know Better:

Name _____

Insta/Snap _____

Name _____

Insta/Snap _____

Name _____

Insta/Snap _____

Name _____

Insta/Snap _____

Got business cards? Staple or paper clip them here:

CAMPUS VISIT #4

INFO SESSION

This section is helpful when you attend the info session. You will most likely learn about:

- Admission requirements, including test scores and important deadlines

- Campus-specific information such as history, on-campus activities and student support services

- Financial aid options and costs associated with attending the university

This may happen before or after the campus tour.

AVERAGES + RATES	
GPA	
SAT	
ACT	
Average Class Size	
Acceptance Rate *How many applicants were admitted?	
Retention Rate *The number of freshmen who returned in year two.	
Graduation Rate *How many students graduate in 6 years?	
Job Placement Rate	

NOTES + OTHER REQUIREMENTS

_____

_____

_____

_____

_____

_____

_____

_____

_____

_____

_____

_____

_____

_____

DEADLINES + THINGS TO KNOW	
Admission Deadlines	
Rolling Admission?	Yes | No
Regular	
Early Action (non-binding) *Students receive an early response to their application	
Early Decision (binding) *Requires student to enroll at admitted school. Generally, you can't withdraw application.	
Scholarship Deadlines	
Separate Scholarship Application Required?	Yes | No
Regular Deadline	
FAFSA Submission Deadlines	
FAFSA Priority Deadline *FAFSA opens October 1	
Date I submitted my FAFSA	

FINANCIAL AID

There are a number of ways to pay for college. The Free Application for Federal Student Aid (FAFSA) (studentaid.ed.gov/sa/fafsa) is required by most colleges and helps determine how much money your family can afford to pay for school.
To complete the form, you will need tax and income information from two years prior.

The FAFSA opens on October 1 and must be completed annually as long as you are enrolled in college.

Some schools may also require you to complete a CSS profile, which is used by some schools only for state and institutional aid (check the resources section for more information).

Let's take a look at the different types of aid:

> LOANS

Borrowed money for college; you must repay your loans, with interest.

> GRANTS & SCHOLARSHIPS

Financial aid that doesn't have to be repaid (unless, for example, you withdraw from school and you will have to forfeit the money.)

> WORK-STUDY

A work program through which you earn money to help you pay for school.

(Source: https://studentaid.ed.gov)

TIP!
Ask your admission counselor about the requirements to be an RA (resident assistant)

OTHER WAYS TO PAY FOR COLLEGE:

1. **Tuition Reimbursement** – your current employer may help cover a portion or all of your education expenses.

2. **Part-time job** – ex. babysitting, server at local restaurant, tutoring at local school.

3. Take **Advanced Placement (AP)** classes in high school and test out of college courses.

EXPENSES

Cost of Attendance: $ _____

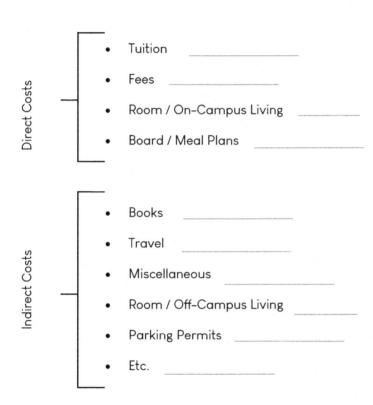

Direct Costs
- Tuition _____
- Fees _____
- Room / On-Campus Living _____
- Board / Meal Plans _____

Indirect Costs
- Books _____
- Travel _____
- Miscellaneous _____
- Room / Off-Campus Living _____
- Parking Permits _____
- Etc. _____

NOTES

_____

_____

_____

_____

CAMPUS VISIT #4

THE ASSESSMENT

The gauges on the next page measure engagement.

Draw an arrow to express how empty or full you feel in regards to each category during the information session and campus tour. For example, during moments of enthusiasm or delight and intense concentration, you may feel more engaged, present in the moment, or full.

Three categories are provided for you, but use the two blank ones to create your own measurements of fullness. Here's an example:

Then, use the notes space to reflect on your feelings in each category.

ENGAGED

DELIVERY OF
INFORMATION

FACILITIES/SPACE

_____

_____

Notes

_____

_____

_____

_____

_____

_____

CAMPUS VISIT #4

LET'S TALK PEOPLE

Use the space on the next page to reflect on the people you meet and see across campus during your tour.

Take notes about your thoughts.

I was impressed by:

_____

_____

I had concerns about:

_____

_____

I'd like more time to talk to:
Use the writing samples in the resource section for pointers!

_____

_____

I'd like to learn more about:
(Majors, Internships, Work-Study Opportunities, Overnight Experiences, etc.)

_____

_____

Professors I met:

_____

_____

Administrators I met:

_____

_____

Overall, students on campus seem to be:

_____

Notable / famous alumni:

_____

_____

Alumni I may know (family, friends, former classmates, etc.):

_____

_____

Today I learned:

_____

_____

_____

CHALLENGE: STEP OUT OF YOUR COMFORT ZONE!

Break the ice with people you meet by asking questions like these. Use the notes pages to jot down their answers!

> What was your greatest challenge in school? It could be related to academics, social, extracurricular, career, etc.

> If you could study abroad anywhere in the world, where would it be?

> Who would you like to trade places with for a week?

> What will you miss most about high school?

> What are you most looking forward to in college?

> How do you define integrity?

> What's your biggest accomplishment?

> If time and money weren't an issue, what kind of business would you have?

NO JOB OR TASK IS TOO SMALL OR BENEATH YOU.

IF YOU WANT TO GET AHEAD, VOLUNTEER TO DO THE THINGS NO ONE ELSE WANTS TO DO, AND DO IT BETTER.

BE A SPONGE. BE OPEN AND LEARN.

- BOBBI BROWN
PROFESSIONAL MAKEUP ARTIST + FOUNDER OF
BOBBI BROWN COSMETICS

COMMENCEMENT SPEAKER - 2014
FASHION INSTITUTE OF TECHNOLOGY

CAMPUS VISIT #4

PERSONAL REFLECTION

Complete this section AFTER your campus visit.

Consider your personality, characteristics, talents, must-haves and goals when completing the questions and scales on the next page as it relates to this college campus visit.

Name of college:

Why am I considering this college?

What really interests me (academic and extracurricular) that's offered here?

How would I describe the campus diversity?

Knowing my must-haves and nice-to-haves, how does this college measure up?

· · · · · · · · · · · ·

Using the scale below, indicate your level of agreement for each "fit" category.

This campus is a realistic...	Strongly Disagree	Disagree	Neither Agree nor Disagree	Agree	Strongly Agree
Academic Fit:	◯	◯	◯	◯	◯
Diversity Fit:	◯	◯	◯	◯	◯
Social Fit:	◯	◯	◯	◯	◯
Financial Fit:	◯	◯	◯	◯	◯
Athletic Fit:	◯	◯	◯	◯	◯
Overall Fit:	◯	◯	◯	◯	◯

· · · · · · · · · · · ·

Next steps for this school:

☐ Start Application　☐ Submit Mid-Year Transcripts　☐ Alumni Interview

☐ Thank You Note　☐ Request More Information　☐ Pay App Fee

☐ Finish Application　☐ Submit FAFSA　☐ Pay Deposit

☐ Other:

CAMPUS VISIT #4

STATUS & PROGRESS

Use the status circles to track your progress for each application deliverable for this university. Once the deliverable is complete, write the completion date in the "100%" circle.

Name of College _____

APPLICATION ○ ○ ○ ○ ○ ○ ○ ○ ○ ○ ○
10%　　　　50%　　　　100%　N/A

ESSAY ○ ○ ○ ○ ○ ○ ○ ○ ○ ○ ○
10%　　　　50%　　　　100%　N/A

TEST SCORE SUBMISSIONS ○ ○ ○ ○ ○ ○ ○ ○ ○ ○ ○
10%　　　　50%　　　　100%　N/A

TEACHER RECS ○ ○ ○ ○ ○ ○ ○ ○ ○ ○ ○
10%　　　　50%　　　　100%　N/A

COUNSELOR RECS ○ ○ ○ ○ ○ ○ ○ ○ ○ ○ ○
10%　　　　50%　　　　100%　N/A

SUPPLEMENT/ EXPRESSION PAGE ○ ○ ○ ○ ○ ○ ○ ○ ○ ○ ○
10%　　　　50%　　　　100%　N/A

FAFSA ○ ○ ○ ○ ○ ○ ○ ○ ○ ○ ○
10%　　　　50%　　　　100%　N/A

SCHOLARSHIP APP #1 ○ ○ ○ ○ ○ ○ ○ ○ ○ ○ ○
10%　　　　50%　　　　100%　N/A

SCHOLARSHIP APP #2 ○ ○ ○ ○ ○ ○ ○ ○ ○ ○ ○
10%　　　　50%　　　　100%　N/A

_____ ○ ○ ○ ○ ○ ○ ○ ○ ○ ○ ○
10%　　　　50%　　　　100%　N/A

BIG IDEAS & RANDOM THOUGHTS

These are bullet pages. Use them as you wish - for notes, to-do lists, to sketch, draw or schedule tasks. Let your imagination drive you.

I'm Curious...

Which of your teachers or school administrators has impacted you the most? Why?

BIG IDEA!
Send this description to your guidance counselor so s/he can use it when writing your letter of recommendation.

NOTES

NOTES

LET'S GO!

CAMPUS VISIT #5

Fill in details about this college using the university's website and brochure or ask an admission counselor.

The next page contains basic facts about the school. Fill in the appropriate spaces and circle the words that best describe the college or university.

You will complete this page for each college campus visit.

DATE: ___/___/___

NAME OF COLLEGE / UNIVERSITY:

_____

 LOCATION + CLOSEST BIG CITY:

_____

NEAREST AIRPORT + MILES FROM HOME:

_____

CAMPUS TYPE: *Circle one*

Rural I Suburban I Urban

 SOCIAL MEDIA HANDLES:

_____

 MASCOT + SCHOOL COLORS:

_____

 STUDENT POPULATION:

_____

 MY DESIRED MAJOR / AREA OF INTEREST:

_____

 INSTITUTION TYPE: *Circle one*

Public I Private

CATEGORY: *Circle one, if applicable*

Historically Black College & University (HBCU) I Men's

Tribal College I Women's I Military I 2-year

Hispanic Serving Institution (HSI) I Religious Affiliation

 ACADEMIC CALENDAR: *Circle one*

Semester I Quarter I Trimester

CAMPUS VISIT #5

ON TOUR + CONTACTS

Take it all in and keep it organized using the checkboxes and prompts on the next few pages to evaluate your experience on campus.

Try to see as much as possible across campus and in the surrounding area and rate it on a scale from 1–5 (5 being the best) to get a good idea of the environment.

Plus, be sure to note the people you meet on campus and your peers on tour. Never underestimate the power of new connections!

If you need more space for notes, remember to use the notes pages at the end of this campus visit section!

I Visited...

- ☐ Student Center
- ☐ Dining Hall
- ☐ Bookstore
- ☐ Library
- ☐ Academic Building
- ☐ Innovation Lab/Center
- ☐ Classroom
- ☐ Rec Center/Gym
- ☐ Athletic Facilities
- ☐ Dorms/Residence Halls
- ☐ Alumni Center
- ☐ Oldest Building
- ☐ Newest Building
- ☐ Local City Attractions
- ☐ Health Center/Clinic
- ☐ Study Spaces
- ☐ Career Center
- ☐ Best Place to Take a Selfie

More On...

> Dorms / Residence Halls

- ☐ Suites / Single Rooms / Shared
- ☐ Co-Ed / All Male / All Female
- ☐ On-Campus Living Requirement: Yes / No
- ☐ Visitation Requirement / Curfew: Yes / No
- ☐ Laundry Fees: Yes / No

> Safety

- ☐ Keycard Access
- ☐ Visible Security / Blue Lights
- ☐ Safety App
- ☐ Self-Defense Training
- ☐ Parking Lots & Access

Now, Let's Rate... (On a scale of 1 to 5 - 5 being the best)

_____ Overall Campus Beauty

_____ Overall Campus Happiness

_____ Greenery/Green space

_____ Plans for Future Campus Growth

_____ ADA Compliant/Accessible Areas*

_____ Green Campus/Recycling Initiatives

_____ Services (Disability, Health Center)

_____ Weather

_____ Traffic: Foot

_____ Traffic: Vehicle

_____ Noise Level

_____ Campus Terrain

_____ Tutoring/Math/Writing Center

_____ My Tour Guide(s)

*Americans with Disabilities Act (ADA) ensures access to the built environment for people with disabilities. See the resources section for more information.

HOLD ON...

Take 30-60 seconds during the tour to quiet your mind and use your five senses to take in the space around you. What do you smell? Hear? Feel? Etc. If you want, close your eyes for better focus.

I'll wait.

My Tour Guide(s):

Name _____   Name _____
✉ Email _____   ✉ Email _____
@ Social Handles _____   @ Social Handles _____
🎓 Class of _____   🎓 Class of _____
◉ Hometown _____   ◉ Hometown _____
🏛 Area of Study _____   🏛 Area of Study _____

My Admission Counselor:

⚲ Name _____
✉ Email _____

Financial Aid Contact:

⚲ Name _____
✉ Email _____

Students I Met + Want To Know Better:

Name _____   Name _____

Insta/Snap _____   Insta/Snap _____

Name _____   Name _____

Insta/Snap _____   Insta/Snap _____

Got business cards? Staple or paper clip them here:

CAMPUS VISIT #5

INFO SESSION

This section is helpful when you attend the info session. You will most likely learn about:

- Admission requirements, including test scores and important deadlines

- Campus-specific information such as history, on-campus activities and student support services

- Financial aid options and costs associated with attending the university

This may happen before or after the campus tour.

AVERAGES + RATES	
GPA	
SAT	
ACT	
Average Class Size	
Acceptance Rate *How many applicants were admitted?*	
Retention Rate *The number of freshmen who returned in year two.*	
Graduation Rate *How many students graduate in 6 years?*	
Job Placement Rate	

NOTES + OTHER REQUIREMENTS

_____

_____

_____

_____

_____

_____

_____

_____

_____

_____

_____

_____

_____

_____

_____

_____

_____

DEADLINES + THINGS TO KNOW	
Admission Deadlines	
Rolling Admission?	Yes | No
Regular	
Early Action (non-binding) *Students receive an early response to their application*	
Early Decision (binding) *Requires student to enroll at admitted school. Generally, you can't withdraw application.*	
Scholarship Deadlines	
Separate Scholarship Application Required?	Yes | No
Regular Deadline	
FAFSA Submission Deadlines	
FAFSA Priority Deadline *FAFSA opens October 1*	
Date I submitted my FAFSA	

FINANCIAL AID

There are a number of ways to pay for college. The Free Application for Federal Student Aid (FAFSA) (studentaid.ed.gov/sa/fafsa) is required by most colleges and helps determine how much money your family can afford to pay for school.
To complete the form, you will need tax and income information from two years prior.

The FAFSA opens on October 1 and must be completed annually as long as you are enrolled in college.

Some schools may also require you to complete a CSS profile, which is used by some schools only for state and institutional aid (check the resources section for more information).

Let's take a look at the different types of aid:

> LOANS

Borrowed money for college; you must repay your loans, with interest.

> GRANTS & SCHOLARSHIPS

Financial aid that doesn't have to be repaid (unless, for example, you withdraw from school and you will have to forfeit the money.)

> WORK-STUDY

A work program through which you earn money to help you pay for school.

(Source: https://studentaid.ed.gov)

TIP!
Ask your admission counselor about the requirements to be an RA (resident assistant)

OTHER WAYS TO PAY FOR COLLEGE:

1. **Tuition Reimbursement** – your current employer may help cover a portion or all of your education expenses.

2. **Part-time job** – ex. babysitting, server at local restaurant, tutoring at local school.

3. Take **Advanced Placement (AP)** classes in high school and test out of college courses.

EXPENSES

Cost of Attendance: $ _____

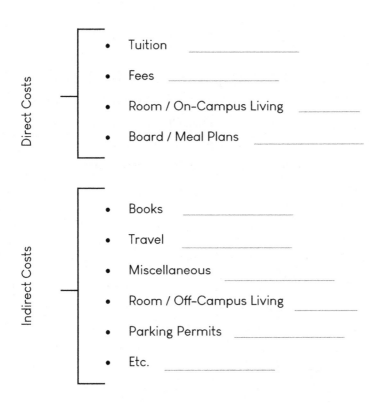

Direct Costs
- Tuition _____
- Fees _____
- Room / On-Campus Living _____
- Board / Meal Plans _____

Indirect Costs
- Books _____
- Travel _____
- Miscellaneous _____
- Room / Off-Campus Living _____
- Parking Permits _____
- Etc. _____

NOTES

_____

_____

_____

_____

_____

THE ASSESSMENT

The gauges on the next page measure engagement.

Draw an arrow to express how empty or full you feel in regards to each category during the information session and campus tour. For example, during moments of enthusiasm or delight and intense concentration, you may feel more engaged, present in the moment, or full.

Three categories are provided for you, but use the two blank ones to create your own measurements of fullness. Here's an example:

Then, use the notes space to reflect on your feelings in each category.

ENGAGED DELIVERY OF INFORMATION FACILITIES/SPACE

Notes

_____

_____

_____

_____

_____

_____

CAMPUS VISIT #5

LET'S TALK PEOPLE

Use the space on the next page to reflect on the people you meet and see across campus during your tour.

Take notes about your thoughts.

I was impressed by:

_____

_____

I had concerns about:

_____

_____

I'd like more time to talk to:
Use the writing samples in the resource section for pointers!

_____

_____

I'd like to learn more about:
(Majors, Internships, Work-Study Opportunities, Overnight Experiences, etc.)

_____

_____

Professors I met:

_____

_____

Administrators I met:

_____

_____

Overall, students on campus seem to be:

_____

Notable / famous alumni:

_____

_____

Alumni I may know (family, friends, former classmates, etc.):

_____

_____

Today I learned:

_____

_____

⚡

CHALLENGE: STEP OUT OF YOUR COMFORT ZONE!

Break the ice with people you meet by asking questions like these. Use the notes pages to jot down their answers!

> What was your greatest challenge in school? It could be related to academics, social, extracurricular, career, etc.

> If you could study abroad anywhere in the world, where would it be?

> Who would you like to trade places with for a week?

> What will you miss most about high school?

> What are you most looking forward to in college?

> How do you define integrity?

> What's your biggest accomplishment?

> If time and money weren't an issue, what kind of business would you have?

I DON'T KNOW WHAT YOUR FUTURE IS, BUT IF YOU'RE WILLING TO TAKE THE HARDER WAY, THE MORE COMPLICATED ONE, THE ONE WITH MORE FAILURES AT FIRST THAN SUCCESSES . . . THEN YOU WILL NOT REGRET IT.

- CHADWICK BOSEMAN, ACTOR

COMMENCEMENT SPEAKER - 2018
HOWARD UNIVERSITY

CAMPUS VISIT #5

PERSONAL REFLECTION

Complete this section AFTER your campus visit.

Consider your personality, characteristics, talents, must-haves and goals when completing the questions and scales on the next page as it relates to this college campus visit.

Name of college:

Why am I considering this college?

What really interests me (academic and extracurricular) that's offered here?

How would I describe the campus diversity?

Knowing my must-haves and nice-to-haves, how does this college measure up?

. . . .

Using the scale below, indicate your level of agreement for each "fit" category.

This campus is a realistic...	Strongly Disagree	Disagree	Neither Agree nor Disagree	Agree	Strongly Agree
Academic Fit:	◯	◯	◯	◯	◯
Diversity Fit:	◯	◯	◯	◯	◯
Social Fit:	◯	◯	◯	◯	◯
Financial Fit:	◯	◯	◯	◯	◯
Athletic Fit:	◯	◯	◯	◯	◯
Overall Fit:	◯	◯	◯	◯	◯

. . . .

Next steps for this school:

- ☐ Start Application
- ☐ Submit Mid-Year Transcripts
- ☐ Alumni Interview
- ☐ Thank You Note
- ☐ Request More Information
- ☐ Pay App Fee
- ☐ Finish Application
- ☐ Submit FAFSA
- ☐ Pay Deposit
- ☐ Other:

CAMPUS VISIT #5

STATUS & PROGRESS

Use the status circles to track your progress for each application deliverable for this university. Once the deliverable is complete, write the completion date in the "100%" circle.

Name of College _____

APPLICATION ⓘ ○ ○ ○ ○ ○ ○ ○ ○ ○ ○ ○
10%　　　　50%　　　　100%　N/A

ESSAY ○ ○ ○ ○ ○ ○ ○ ○ ○ ○ ○
10%　　　　50%　　　　100%　N/A

TEST SCORE
SUBMISSIONS ○ ○ ○ ○ ○ ○ ○ ○ ○ ○ ○
10%　　　　50%　　　　100%　N/A

TEACHER RECS ○ ○ ○ ○ ○ ○ ○ ○ ○ ○ ○
10%　　　　50%　　　　100%　N/A

COUNSELOR
RECS ○ ○ ○ ○ ○ ○ ○ ○ ○ ○ ○
10%　　　　50%　　　　100%　N/A

SUPPLEMENT/
EXPRESSION PAGE ○ ○ ○ ○ ○ ○ ○ ○ ○ ○ ○
10%　　　　50%　　　　100%　N/A

FAFSA ○ ○ ○ ○ ○ ○ ○ ○ ○ ○ ○
10%　　　　50%　　　　100%　N/A

SCHOLARSHIP
APP #1 ○ ○ ○ ○ ○ ○ ○ ○ ○ ○ ○
10%　　　　50%　　　　100%　N/A

SCHOLARSHIP
APP #2 ○ ○ ○ ○ ○ ○ ○ ○ ○ ○ ○
10%　　　　50%　　　　100%　N/A

_____ ○ ○ ○ ○ ○ ○ ○ ○ ○ ○ ○
10%　　　　50%　　　　100%　N/A

BIG IDEAS & RANDOM THOUGHTS

These are bullet pages. Use them as you wish - for notes, to-do lists, to sketch, draw or schedule tasks. Let your imagination drive you.

I'm Curious...

How would your parents and/or family members describe you?

NOTES

NOTES

GET YOUR PEN READY...

CAMPUS VISIT #6

Fill in details about this college using the university's website and brochure or ask an admission counselor.

The next page contains basic facts about the school. Fill in the appropriate spaces and circle the words that best describe the college or university.

You will complete this page for each college campus visit.

DATE: ___ / ___ / ___

NAME OF COLLEGE / UNIVERSITY:

_____

LOCATION + CLOSEST BIG CITY:

_____

NEAREST AIRPORT + MILES FROM HOME:

_____

CAMPUS TYPE: *Circle one*

Rural | Suburban | Urban

SOCIAL MEDIA HANDLES:

_____

MASCOT + SCHOOL COLORS:

_____

STUDENT POPULATION:

_____

MY DESIRED MAJOR / AREA OF INTEREST:

_____

INSTITUTION TYPE: *Circle one*

Public | Private

CATEGORY: *Circle one, if applicable*

Historically Black College & University (HBCU) | Men's

Tribal College | Women's | Military | 2-year

Hispanic Serving Institution (HSI) | Religious Affiliation

ACADEMIC CALENDAR: *Circle one*

Semester | Quarter | Trimester

CAMPUS VISIT #6

ON TOUR + CONTACTS

Take it all in and keep it organized using the checkboxes and prompts on the next few pages to evaluate your experience on campus.

Try to see as much as possible across campus and in the surrounding area and rate it on a scale from 1–5 (5 being the best) to get a good idea of the environment.

Plus, be sure to note the people you meet on campus and your peers on tour. Never underestimate the power of new connections!

If you need more space for notes, remember to use the notes pages at the end of this campus visit section!

I Visited...

☐ Student Center ☐ Classroom ☐ Newest Building

☐ Dining Hall ☐ Rec Center/Gym ☐ Local City Attractions

☐ Bookstore ☐ Athletic Facilities ☐ Health Center/Clinic

☐ Library ☐ Dorms/Residence Halls ☐ Study Spaces

☐ Academic Building ☐ Alumni Center ☐ Career Center

☐ Innovation Lab/Center ☐ Oldest Building ☐ Best Place to Take a Selfie

More On...

> Dorms / Residence Halls

☐ Suites / Single Rooms / Shared

☐ Co-Ed / All Male / All Female

☐ On-Campus Living Requirement: Yes / No

☐ Visitation Requirement / Curfew: Yes / No

☐ Laundry Fees: Yes / No

> Safety

☐ Keycard Access

☐ Visible Security / Blue Lights

☐ Safety App

☐ Self-Defense Training

☐ Parking Lots & Access

Now, Let's Rate... (On a scale of 1 to 5 – 5 being the best)

_____ Overall Campus Beauty

_____ Overall Campus Happiness

_____ Greenery/Green space

_____ Plans for Future Campus Growth

_____ ADA Compliant/Accessible Areas*

_____ Green Campus/Recycling Initiatives

_____ Services (Disability, Health Center)

_____ Weather

_____ Traffic: Foot

_____ Traffic: Vehicle

_____ Noise Level

_____ Campus Terrain

_____ Tutoring/Math/Writing Center

_____ My Tour Guide(s)

*Americans with Disabilities Act (ADA) ensures access to the built environment for people with disabilities. See the resources section for more information.

HOLD ON...

Take 30-60 seconds during the tour to quiet your mind and use your five senses to take in the space around you. What do you smell? Hear? Feel? Etc. If you want, close your eyes for better focus.

I'll wait.

My Tour Guide(s):

Name _____   Name _____

✉ Email _____   ✉ Email _____

@ Social Handles _____   @ Social Handles _____

🎓 Class of _____   🎓 Class of _____

📍 Hometown _____   📍 Hometown _____

🏛 Area of Study _____   🏛 Area of Study _____

My Admission Counselor:

👤 Name _____

✉ Email _____

Financial Aid Contact:

👤 Name _____

✉ Email _____

Students I Met + Want To Know Better:

Name _____   Name _____

Insta/Snap _____   Insta/Snap _____

Name _____   Name _____

Insta/Snap _____   Insta/Snap _____

Got business cards? Staple or paper clip them here:

CAMPUS VISIT #6

INFO SESSION

This section is helpful when you attend the info session. You will most likely learn about:

- Admission requirements, including test scores and important deadlines

- Campus-specific information such as history, on-campus activities and student support services

- Financial aid options and costs associated with attending the university

This may happen before or after the campus tour.

AVERAGES + RATES	
GPA	
SAT	
ACT	
Average Class Size	
Acceptance Rate *How many applicants were admitted?*	
Retention Rate *The number of freshmen who returned in year two.*	
Graduation Rate *How many students graduate in 6 years?*	
Job Placement Rate	

NOTES + OTHER REQUIREMENTS

_____

_____

_____

_____

_____

_____

_____

_____

_____

_____

_____

_____

_____

DEADLINES + THINGS TO KNOW	
Admission Deadlines	
Rolling Admission?	Yes | No
Regular	
Early Action (non-binding) *Students receive an early response to their application*	
Early Decision (binding) *Requires student to enroll at admitted school. Generally, you can't withdraw application.*	
Scholarship Deadlines	
Separate Scholarship Application Required?	Yes | No
Regular Deadline	
FAFSA Submission Deadlines	
FAFSA Priority Deadline *FAFSA opens October 1*	
Date I submitted my FAFSA	

FINANCIAL AID

There are a number of ways to pay for college. The Free Application for Federal Student Aid (FAFSA) (studentaid.ed.gov/sa/fafsa) is required by most colleges and helps determine how much money your family can afford to pay for school.
To complete the form, you will need tax and income information from two years prior.

The FAFSA opens on October 1 and must be completed annually as long as you are enrolled in college.

Some schools may also require you to complete a CSS profile, which is used by some schools only for state and institutional aid (check the resources section for more information).

Let's take a look at the different types of aid:

> LOANS
Borrowed money for college; you must repay your loans, with interest.

> GRANTS & SCHOLARSHIPS
Financial aid that doesn't have to be repaid (unless, for example, you withdraw from school and you will have to forfeit the money.)

> WORK-STUDY
A work program through which you earn money to help you pay for school.

(Source: https://studentaid.ed.gov)

TIP!
Ask your admission counselor about the requirements to be an RA (resident assistant)

OTHER WAYS TO PAY FOR COLLEGE:

1. **Tuition Reimbursement** – your current employer may help cover a portion or all of your education expenses.

2. **Part-time job** – ex. babysitting, server at local restaurant, tutoring at local school.

3. Take **Advanced Placement (AP)** classes in high school and test out of college courses.

EXPENSES

Cost of Attendance: $ _____

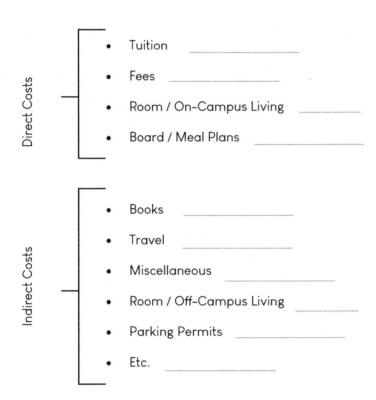

Direct Costs

- Tuition _____
- Fees _____
- Room / On-Campus Living _____
- Board / Meal Plans _____

Indirect Costs

- Books _____
- Travel _____
- Miscellaneous _____
- Room / Off-Campus Living _____
- Parking Permits _____
- Etc. _____

NOTES

_____

_____

_____

_____

CAMPUS VISIT #6

THE ASSESSMENT

The gauges on the next page measure engagement.

Draw an arrow to express how empty or full you feel in regards to each category during the information session and campus tour. For example, during moments of enthusiasm or delight and intense concentration, you may feel more engaged, present in the moment, or full.

Three categories are provided for you, but use the two blank ones to create your own measurements of fullness. Here's an example:

Then, use the notes space to reflect on your feelings in each category.

Notes

_____

_____

_____

_____

_____

CAMPUS VISIT #6

LET'S TALK PEOPLE

Use the space on the next page to reflect on the people you meet and see across campus during your tour.

Take notes about your thoughts.

I was impressed by:

_____

_____

I had concerns about:

_____

_____

I'd like more time to talk to:
Use the writing samples in the resource section for pointers!

_____

_____

I'd like to learn more about:
(Majors, Internships, Work-Study Opportunities, Overnight Experiences, etc.)

_____

_____

Professors I met:

_____

_____

Administrators I met:

_____

_____

Overall, students on campus seem to be:

_____

Notable / famous alumni:

_____

_____

Alumni I may know (family, friends, former classmates, etc.):

_____

_____

Today I learned:

_____

_____

⚡

CHALLENGE: STEP OUT OF YOUR COMFORT ZONE!

Break the ice with people you meet by asking questions like these. Use the notes pages to jot down their answers!

> What was your greatest challenge in school? It could be related to academics, social, extracurricular, career, etc.

> If you could study abroad anywhere in the world, where would it be?

> Who would you like to trade places with for a week?

> What will you miss most about high school?

> What are you most looking forward to in college?

> How do you define integrity?

> What's your biggest accomplishment?

> If time and money weren't an issue, what kind of business would you have?

IF YOU WANT TO TAKE CREDIT, FIRST LEARN TO TAKE RESPONSIBILITY.

- TIM COOK, CEO, APPLE

COMMENCEMENT SPEAKER – 2019
STANFORD UNIVERSITY

CAMPUS VISIT #6

PERSONAL REFLECTION

Complete this section AFTER your campus visit.

Consider your personality, characteristics, talents, must-haves and goals when completing the questions and scales on the next page as it relates to this college campus visit.

Name of college:

_____

Why am I considering this college?

_____

What really interests me (academic and extracurricular) that's offered here?

_____

How would I describe the campus diversity?

_____

Knowing my must-haves and nice-to-haves, how does this college measure up?

_____

· · · · · · · · · · · ·

Using the scale below, indicate your level of agreement for each "fit" category.

This campus is a realistic...	Strongly Disagree	Disagree	Neither Agree nor Disagree	Agree	Strongly Agree
Academic Fit:	◯	◯	◯	◯	◯
Diversity Fit:	◯	◯	◯	◯	◯
Social Fit:	◯	◯	◯	◯	◯
Financial Fit:	◯	◯	◯	◯	◯
Athletic Fit:	◯	◯	◯	◯	◯
Overall Fit:	◯	◯	◯	◯	◯

· · · · · · · · · · · ·

Next steps for this school:

- ☐ Start Application
- ☐ Submit Mid-Year Transcripts
- ☐ Alumni Interview
- ☐ Thank You Note
- ☐ Request More Information
- ☐ Pay App Fee
- ☐ Finish Application
- ☐ Submit FAFSA
- ☐ Pay Deposit
- ☐ Other:

CAMPUS VISIT #6

STATUS & PROGRESS

Use the status circles to track your progress for each application deliverable for this university. Once the deliverable is complete, write the completion date in the "100%" circle.

Name of College _____

APPLICATION ○ ○ ○ ○ ○ ○ ○ ○ ○ ○ ○
10%   50%   100% N/A

ESSAY ○ ○ ○ ○ ○ ○ ○ ○ ○ ○ ○
10%   50%   100% N/A

TEST SCORE SUBMISSIONS ○ ○ ○ ○ ○ ○ ○ ○ ○ ○ ○
10%   50%   100% N/A

TEACHER RECS ○ ○ ○ ○ ○ ○ ○ ○ ○ ○ ○
10%   50%   100% N/A

COUNSELOR RECS ○ ○ ○ ○ ○ ○ ○ ○ ○ ○ ○
10%   50%   100% N/A

SUPPLEMENT/ EXPRESSION PAGE ○ ○ ○ ○ ○ ○ ○ ○ ○ ○ ○
10%   50%   100% N/A

FAFSA ○ ○ ○ ○ ○ ○ ○ ○ ○ ○ ○
10%   50%   100% N/A

SCHOLARSHIP APP #1 ○ ○ ○ ○ ○ ○ ○ ○ ○ ○ ○
10%   50%   100% N/A

SCHOLARSHIP APP #2 ○ ○ ○ ○ ○ ○ ○ ○ ○ ○ ○
10%   50%   100% N/A

_____ ○ ○ ○ ○ ○ ○ ○ ○ ○ ○ ○
10%   50%   100% N/A

BIG IDEAS & RANDOM THOUGHTS

These are bullet pages. Use them as you wish - for notes, to-do lists, to sketch, draw or schedule tasks. Let your imagination drive you.

I'm Curious...

What's your definition of success? What's the dictionary's definition? What differences/similarities do you see between the two definitions?

BIG IDEA!
Send this description to your guidance counselor so s/he can use it when writing your letter of recommendation.

NOTES

NOTES

NO ONE KNOWS YOU LIKE YOU DO!

CAMPUS VISIT #7

Fill in details about this college using the university's website and brochure or ask an admission counselor.

The next page contains basic facts about the school. Fill in the appropriate spaces and circle the words that best describe the college or university.

You will complete this page for each college campus visit.

NAME OF COLLEGE / UNIVERSITY:

_____

LOCATION + CLOSEST BIG CITY:

_____

NEAREST AIRPORT + MILES FROM HOME:

_____

CAMPUS TYPE: *Circle one*

Rural I Suburban I Urban

SOCIAL MEDIA HANDLES:

_____

MASCOT + SCHOOL COLORS:

_____

STUDENT POPULATION:

_____

MY DESIRED MAJOR / AREA OF INTEREST:

_____

INSTITUTION TYPE: *Circle one*

Public I Private

CATEGORY: *Circle one, if applicable*

Historically Black College & University (HBCU) I Men's

Tribal College I Women's I Military I 2-year

Hispanic Serving Institution (HSI) I Religious Affiliation

ACADEMIC CALENDAR: *Circle one*

Semester I Quarter I Trimester

CAMPUS VISIT #7

ON TOUR + CONTACTS

Take it all in and keep it organized using the checkboxes and prompts on the next few pages to evaluate your experience on campus.

Try to see as much as possible across campus and in the surrounding area and rate it on a scale from 1-5 (5 being the best) to get a good idea of the environment.

Plus, be sure to note the people you meet on campus and your peers on tour. Never underestimate the power of new connections!

If you need more space for notes, remember to use the notes pages at the end of this campus visit section!

I Visited...

- ☐ Student Center
- ☐ Dining Hall
- ☐ Bookstore
- ☐ Library
- ☐ Academic Building
- ☐ Innovation Lab/Center
- ☐ Classroom
- ☐ Rec Center/Gym
- ☐ Athletic Facilities
- ☐ Dorms/Residence Halls
- ☐ Alumni Center
- ☐ Oldest Building
- ☐ Newest Building
- ☐ Local City Attractions
- ☐ Health Center/Clinic
- ☐ Study Spaces
- ☐ Career Center
- ☐ Best Place to Take a Selfie

More On...

> Dorms / Residence Halls

- ☐ Suites / Single Rooms / Shared
- ☐ Co-Ed / All Male / All Female
- ☐ On-Campus Living Requirement: Yes / No
- ☐ Visitation Requirement / Curfew: Yes / No
- ☐ Laundry Fees: Yes / No

> Safety

- ☐ Keycard Access
- ☐ Visible Security / Blue Lights
- ☐ Safety App
- ☐ Self-Defense Training
- ☐ Parking Lots & Access

Now, Let's Rate... (On a scale of 1 to 5 - 5 being the best)

_____ Overall Campus Beauty

_____ Overall Campus Happiness

_____ Greenery/Green space

_____ Plans for Future Campus Growth

_____ ADA Compliant/Accessible Areas*

_____ Green Campus/Recycling Initiatives

_____ Services (Disability, Health Center)

_____ Weather

_____ Traffic: Foot

_____ Traffic: Vehicle

_____ Noise Level

_____ Campus Terrain

_____ Tutoring/Math/Writing Center

_____ My Tour Guide(s)

*Americans with Disabilities Act (ADA) ensures access to the built environment for people with disabilities. See the resources section for more information.

HOLD ON...

Take 30-60 seconds during the tour to quiet your mind and use your five senses to take in the space around you. What do you smell? Hear? Feel? Etc. If you want, close your eyes for better focus.

I'll wait.

My Tour Guide(s):

Name _____   Name _____
✉ Email _____   ✉ Email _____
@ Social Handles _____   @ Social Handles _____
🎓 Class of _____   🎓 Class of _____
◎ Hometown _____   ◎ Hometown _____
🏫 Area of Study _____   🏫 Area of Study _____

My Admission Counselor:

👤 Name _____
✉ Email _____

Financial Aid Contact:

👤 Name _____
✉ Email _____

Students I Met + Want To Know Better:

Name _____   Name _____

Insta/Snap _____   Insta/Snap _____

Name _____   Name _____

Insta/Snap _____   Insta/Snap _____

Got business cards? Staple or paper clip them here:

CAMPUS VISIT #7

INFO SESSION

This section is helpful when you attend the info session. You will most likely learn about:

- Admission requirements, including test scores and important deadlines

- Campus-specific information such as history, on-campus activities and student support services

- Financial aid options and costs associated with attending the university

This may happen before or after the campus tour.

AVERAGES + RATES	
GPA	
SAT	
ACT	
Average Class Size	
Acceptance Rate *How many applicants were admitted?*	
Retention Rate *The number of freshmen who returned in year two.*	
Graduation Rate *How many students graduate in 6 years?*	
Job Placement Rate	

NOTES + OTHER REQUIREMENTS

DEADLINES + THINGS TO KNOW	
Admission Deadlines	
Rolling Admission?	Yes I No
Regular	
Early Action (non-binding) *Students receive an early response to their application*	
Early Decision (binding) *Requires student to enroll at admitted school. Generally, you can't withdraw application.*	
Scholarship Deadlines	
Separate Scholarship Application Required?	Yes I No
Regular Deadline	
FAFSA Submission Deadlines	
FAFSA Priority Deadline *FAFSA opens October 1*	
Date I submitted my FAFSA	

FINANCIAL AID

There are a number of ways to pay for college. The Free Application for Federal Student Aid (FAFSA) (studentaid.ed.gov/sa/fafsa) is required by most colleges and helps determine how much money your family can afford to pay for school.
To complete the form, you will need tax and income information from two years prior.

The FAFSA opens on October 1 and must be completed annually as long as you are enrolled in college.

Some schools may also require you to complete a CSS profile, which is used by some schools only for state and institutional aid (check the resources section for more information).

Let's take a look at the different types of aid:

> LOANS
Borrowed money for college; you must repay your loans, with interest.

> GRANTS & SCHOLARSHIPS
Financial aid that doesn't have to be repaid (unless, for example, you withdraw from school and you will have to forfeit the money.)

> WORK-STUDY
A work program through which you earn money to help you pay for school.

(Source: https://studentaid.ed.gov)

TIP!
Ask your admission counselor about the requirements to be an RA (resident assistant)

OTHER WAYS TO PAY FOR COLLEGE:

1. **Tuition Reimbursement** – your current employer may help cover a portion or all of your education expenses.

2. **Part-time job** – ex. babysitting, server at local restaurant, tutoring at local school.

3. Take **Advanced Placement (AP)** classes in high school and test out of college courses.

EXPENSES

Cost of Attendance: $ _____

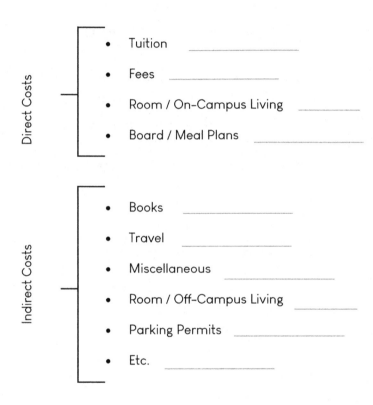

Direct Costs
- Tuition _____
- Fees _____
- Room / On-Campus Living _____
- Board / Meal Plans _____

Indirect Costs
- Books _____
- Travel _____
- Miscellaneous _____
- Room / Off-Campus Living _____
- Parking Permits _____
- Etc. _____

NOTES

_____

_____

_____

_____

CAMPUS VISIT #7

THE ASSESSMENT

The gauges on the next page measure engagement.

Draw an arrow to express how empty or full you feel in regards to each category during the information session and campus tour. For example, during moments of enthusiasm or delight and intense concentration, you may feel more engaged, present in the moment, or full.

Three categories are provided for you, but use the two blank ones to create your own measurements of fullness. Here's an example:

Then, use the notes space to reflect on your feelings in each category.

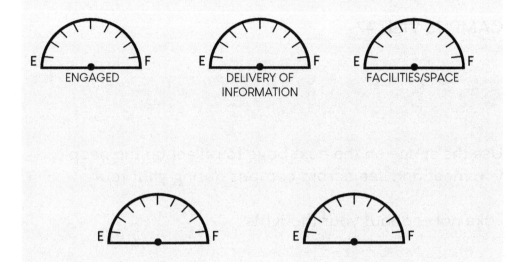

ENGAGED

DELIVERY OF
INFORMATION

FACILITIES/SPACE

Notes

_____

_____

_____

_____

_____

_____

CAMPUS VISIT #7

LET'S TALK PEOPLE

Use the space on the next page to reflect on the people you meet and see across campus during your tour.

Take notes about your thoughts.

I was impressed by:

_____

_____

I had concerns about:

_____

_____

I'd like more time to talk to:
Use the writing samples in the resource section for pointers!

_____

_____

I'd like to learn more about:
(Majors, Internships, Work-Study Opportunities, Overnight Experiences, etc.)

_____

_____

Professors I met:

_____

_____

Administrators I met:

_____

_____

Overall, students on campus seem to be:

_____

Notable / famous alumni:

_____

_____

Alumni I may know (family, friends, former classmates, etc.):

_____

_____

Today I learned:

_____

_____

CHALLENGE: STEP OUT OF YOUR COMFORT ZONE!

Break the ice with people you meet by asking questions like these. Use the notes pages to jot down their answers!

> What was your greatest challenge in school? It could be related to academics, social, extracurricular, career, etc.

> If you could study abroad anywhere in the world, where would it be?

> Who would you like to trade places with for a week?

> What will you miss most about high school?

> What are you most looking forward to in college?

> How do you define integrity?

> What's your biggest accomplishment?

> If time and money weren't an issue, what kind of business would you have?

OFTEN IT'S THE ADVERSITY IN YOUR LIFE THAT GIVES YOU THE GREATEST IDEAS.

- KATHRINE SWITZER
THE FIRST WOMAN TO RUN IN THE BOSTON MARATHON IN 1967

COMMENCEMENT SPEAKER - 2018
SYRACUSE UNIVERSITY

CAMPUS VISIT #7

PERSONAL REFLECTION

Complete this section AFTER your campus visit.

Consider your personality, characteristics, talents, must-haves and goals when completing the questions and scales on the next page as it relates to this college campus visit.

Name of college:

Why am I considering this college?

What really interests me (academic and extracurricular) that's offered here?

How would I describe the campus diversity?

Knowing my must-haves and nice-to-haves, how does this college measure up?

· · · · · · · · · · · · ·

Using the scale below, indicate your level of agreement for each "fit" category.

This campus is a realistic...	Strongly Disagree	Disagree	Neither Agree nor Disagree	Agree	Strongly Agree
Academic Fit:	○	○	○	○	○
Diversity Fit:	○	○	○	○	○
Social Fit:	○	○	○	○	○
Financial Fit:	○	○	○	○	○
Athletic Fit:	○	○	○	○	○
Overall Fit:	○	○	○	○	○

· · · · · · · · · · · · ·

Next steps for this school:

☐ Start Application ☐ Submit Mid-Year Transcripts ☐ Alumni Interview

☐ Thank You Note ☐ Request More Information ☐ Pay App Fee

☐ Finish Application ☐ Submit FAFSA ☐ Pay Deposit

☐ Other:

CAMPUS VISIT #7

STATUS & PROGRESS

Use the status circles to track your progress for each application deliverable for this university. Once the deliverable is complete, write the completion date in the "100%" circle.

Name of College _____

APPLICATION   ○ ○ ○ ○ ○ ○ ○ ○ ○ ○ ○
10%   50%   100% N/A

ESSAY   ○ ○ ○ ○ ○ ○ ○ ○ ○ ○ ○
10%   50%   100% N/A

TEST SCORE
SUBMISSIONS   ○ ○ ○ ○ ○ ○ ○ ○ ○ ○ ○
10%   50%   100% N/A

TEACHER RECS   ○ ○ ○ ○ ○ ○ ○ ○ ○ ○ ○
10%   50%   100% N/A

COUNSELOR
RECS   ○ ○ ○ ○ ○ ○ ○ ○ ○ ○ ○
10%   50%   100% N/A

SUPPLEMENT/
EXPRESSION PAGE   ○ ○ ○ ○ ○ ○ ○ ○ ○ ○ ○
10%   50%   100% N/A

FAFSA   ○ ○ ○ ○ ○ ○ ○ ○ ○ ○ ○
10%   50%   100% N/A

SCHOLARSHIP
APP #1   ○ ○ ○ ○ ○ ○ ○ ○ ○ ○ ○
10%   50%   100% N/A

SCHOLARSHIP
APP #2   ○ ○ ○ ○ ○ ○ ○ ○ ○ ○ ○
10%   50%   100% N/A

_____   ○ ○ ○ ○ ○ ○ ○ ○ ○ ○ ○
10%   50%   100% N/A

BIG IDEAS & RANDOM THOUGHTS

These are bullet pages. Use them as you wish - for notes, to-do lists, to sketch, draw or schedule tasks. Let your imagination drive you.

I'm Curious...

What would you do if you won a billion dollars in the lottery? Be specific!

NOTES

NOTES

GO FOR IT!

CAMPUS VISIT #8

Fill in details about this college using the university's website and brochure or ask an admission counselor.

The next page contains basic facts about the school. Fill in the appropriate spaces and circle the words that best describe the college or university.

You will complete this page for each college campus visit.

DATE: ___ / ___ / ___

NAME OF COLLEGE / UNIVERSITY:
_____

LOCATION + CLOSEST BIG CITY:
_____

NEAREST AIRPORT + MILES FROM HOME:
_____

CAMPUS TYPE: *Circle one*

Rural | Suburban | Urban

SOCIAL MEDIA HANDLES:
_____

MASCOT + SCHOOL COLORS:
_____

STUDENT POPULATION:
_____

MY DESIRED MAJOR / AREA OF INTEREST:
_____

INSTITUTION TYPE: *Circle one*

Public | Private

CATEGORY: *Circle one, if applicable*

Historically Black College & University (HBCU) | Men's

Tribal College | Women's | Military | 2-year

Hispanic Serving Institution (HSI) | Religious Affiliation

ACADEMIC CALENDAR: *Circle one*

Semester | Quarter | Trimester

CAMPUS VISIT #8

ON TOUR + CONTACTS

Take it all in and keep it organized using the checkboxes and prompts on the next few pages to evaluate your experience on campus.

Try to see as much as possible across campus and in the surrounding area and rate it on a scale from 1-5 (5 being the best) to get a good idea of the environment.

Plus, be sure to note the people you meet on campus and your peers on tour. Never underestimate the power of new connections!

If you need more space for notes, remember to use the notes pages at the end of this campus visit section!

I Visited...

- ☐ Student Center
- ☐ Dining Hall
- ☐ Bookstore
- ☐ Library
- ☐ Academic Building
- ☐ Innovation Lab/Center
- ☐ Classroom
- ☐ Rec Center/Gym
- ☐ Athletic Facilities
- ☐ Dorms/Residence Halls
- ☐ Alumni Center
- ☐ Oldest Building
- ☐ Newest Building
- ☐ Local City Attractions
- ☐ Health Center/Clinic
- ☐ Study Spaces
- ☐ Career Center
- ☐ Best Place to Take a Selfie

More On...

> **Dorms / Residence Halls**

- ☐ Suites / Single Rooms / Shared
- ☐ Co-Ed / All Male / All Female
- ☐ On-Campus Living Requirement: Yes / No
- ☐ Visitation Requirement / Curfew: Yes / No
- ☐ Laundry Fees: Yes / No

> **Safety**

- ☐ Keycard Access
- ☐ Visible Security / Blue Lights
- ☐ Safety App
- ☐ Self-Defense Training
- ☐ Parking Lots & Access

Now, Let's Rate... (On a scale of 1 to 5 - 5 being the best)

_____ Overall Campus Beauty

_____ Overall Campus Happiness

_____ Greenery/Green space

_____ Plans for Future Campus Growth

_____ ADA Compliant/Accessible Areas*

_____ Green Campus/Recycling Initiatives

_____ Services (Disability, Health Center)

_____ Weather

_____ Traffic: Foot

_____ Traffic: Vehicle

_____ Noise Level

_____ Campus Terrain

_____ Tutoring/Math/Writing Center

_____ My Tour Guide(s)

*Americans with Disabilities Act (ADA) ensures access to the built environment for people with disabilities. See the resources section for more information.

HOLD ON...

Take 30-60 seconds during the tour to quiet your mind and use your five senses to take in the space around you. What do you smell? Hear? Feel? Etc. If you want, close your eyes for better focus.

I'll wait.

My Tour Guide(s):

Name _____   Name _____

✉ Email _____   ✉ Email _____

@ Social Handles _____   @ Social Handles _____

🎓 Class of _____   🎓 Class of _____

📍 Hometown _____   📍 Hometown _____

🏫 Area of Study _____   🏫 Area of Study _____

My Admission Counselor:

👤 Name _____

✉ Email _____

Financial Aid Contact:

👤 Name _____

✉ Email _____

Students I Met + Want To Know Better:

Name _____   Name _____

Insta/Snap _____   Insta/Snap _____

Name _____   Name _____

Insta/Snap _____   Insta/Snap _____

Got business cards? Staple or paper clip them here:

CAMPUS VISIT #8

INFO SESSION

This section is helpful when you attend the info session. You will most likely learn about:

- Admission requirements, including test scores and important deadlines

- Campus-specific information such as history, on-campus activities and student support services

- Financial aid options and costs associated with attending the university

This may happen before or after the campus tour.

AVERAGES + RATES	
GPA	
SAT	
ACT	
Average Class Size	
Acceptance Rate *How many applicants were admitted?	
Retention Rate *The number of freshmen who returned in year two.	
Graduation Rate *How many students graduate in 6 years?	
Job Placement Rate	

NOTES + OTHER REQUIREMENTS

_____

_____

_____

_____

_____

_____

_____

_____

_____

_____

_____

_____

_____

_____

DEADLINES + THINGS TO KNOW	
Admission Deadlines	
Rolling Admission?	Yes | No
Regular	
Early Action (non-binding) *Students receive an early response to their application	
Early Decision (binding) *Requires student to enroll at admitted school. Generally, you can't withdraw application.	
Scholarship Deadlines	
Separate Scholarship Application Required?	Yes | No
Regular Deadline	
FAFSA Submission Deadlines	
FAFSA Priority Deadline *FAFSA opens October 1	
Date I submitted my FAFSA	

FINANCIAL AID

There are a number of ways to pay for college. The Free Application for Federal Student Aid (FAFSA) (studentaid.ed.gov/sa/fafsa) is required by most colleges and helps determine how much money your family can afford to pay for school.
To complete the form, you will need tax and income information from two years prior.

The FAFSA opens on October 1 and must be completed annually as long as you are enrolled in college.

Some schools may also require you to complete a CSS profile, which is used by some schools only for state and institutional aid (check the resources section for more information).

Let's take a look at the different types of aid:

> LOANS

Borrowed money for college; you must repay your loans, with interest.

> GRANTS & SCHOLARSHIPS

Financial aid that doesn't have to be repaid (unless, for example, you withdraw from school and you will have to forfeit the money.)

> WORK-STUDY

A work program through which you earn money to help you pay for school.

(Source: https://studentaid.ed.gov)

TIP!
Ask your admission counselor about the requirements to be an RA (resident assistant)

OTHER WAYS TO PAY FOR COLLEGE:

1. **Tuition Reimbursement** - your current employer may help cover a portion or all of your education expenses.

2. **Part-time job** - ex. babysitting, server at local restaurant, tutoring at local school.

3. Take **Advanced Placement (AP)** classes in high school and test out of college courses.

EXPENSES

Cost of Attendance: $ _____

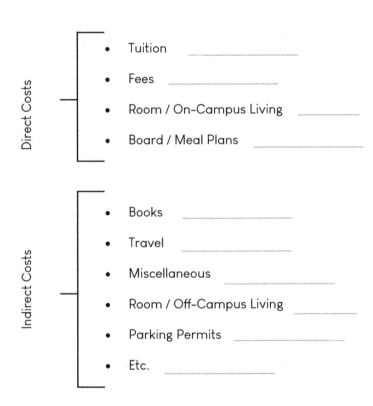

Direct Costs

- Tuition _____
- Fees _____
- Room / On-Campus Living _____
- Board / Meal Plans _____

Indirect Costs

- Books _____
- Travel _____
- Miscellaneous _____
- Room / Off-Campus Living _____
- Parking Permits _____
- Etc. _____

NOTES

_____

_____

_____

_____

CAMPUS VISIT #8

THE ASSESSMENT

The gauges on the next page measure engagement.

Draw an arrow to express how empty or full you feel in regards to each category during the information session and campus tour. For example, during moments of enthusiasm or delight and intense concentration, you may feel more engaged, present in the moment, or full.

Three categories are provided for you, but use the two blank ones to create your own measurements of fullness. Here's an example:

Then, use the notes space to reflect on your feelings in each category.

Notes

_____

_____

_____

_____

_____

_____

LET'S TALK PEOPLE

Use the space on the next page to reflect on the people you meet and see across campus during your tour.

Take notes about your thoughts.

I was impressed by:

_____

_____

I had concerns about:

_____

_____

I'd like more time to talk to:
Use the writing samples in the resource section for pointers!

_____

_____

I'd like to learn more about:
(Majors, Internships, Work-Study Opportunities, Overnight Experiences, etc.)

_____

_____

Professors I met:

_____

_____

Administrators I met:

_____

_____

Overall, students on campus seem to be:

_____

Notable / famous alumni:

_____

_____

Alumni I may know (family, friends, former classmates, etc.):

_____

_____

Today I learned:

_____

_____

CHALLENGE: STEP OUT OF YOUR COMFORT ZONE!

Break the ice with people you meet by asking questions like these. Use the notes pages to jot down their answers!

> What was your greatest challenge in school? It could be related to academics, social, extracurricular, career, etc.

> If you could study abroad anywhere in the world, where would it be?

> Who would you like to trade places with for a week?

> What will you miss most about high school?

> What are you most looking forward to in college?

> How do you define integrity?

> What's your biggest accomplishment?

> If time and money weren't an issue, what kind of business would you have?

AND FINALLY, THIS: THIS WILL SAVE YOU. STOP COMPARING YOURSELF TO OTHER PEOPLE. YOU'RE ONLY ON THIS PLANET TO BE YOU, NOT SOMEONE ELSE'S IMITATION OF YOU...YOUR LIFE JOURNEY IS ABOUT LEARNING TO BECOME MORE OF WHO YOU ARE AND FULFILLING THE HIGHEST, TRUEST EXPRESSION OF YOURSELF AS A HUMAN BEING. THAT'S WHY YOU'RE HERE. YOU WILL DO THAT THROUGH YOUR WORK AND YOUR ART, THROUGH YOUR RELATIONSHIPS AND LOVE.

- OPRAH WINFREY
TELEVISION PIONEER + ACTRESS + MEDIA EXECUTIVE AND PHILANTHROPIST

COMMENCEMENT SPEAKER - 2018
UNIVERSITY OF SOUTHERN CALIFORNIA
ANNENBERG SCHOOL FOR COMMUNICATION AND JOURNALISM

PERSONAL REFLECTION

Complete this section AFTER your campus visit.

Consider your personality, characteristics, talents, must-haves and goals when completing the questions and scales on the next page as it relates to this college campus visit.

Name of college:

Why am I considering this college?

What really interests me (academic and extracurricular) that's offered here?

How would I describe the campus diversity?

Knowing my must-haves and nice-to-haves, how does this college measure up?

• • • • • • • • • • • • •

Using the scale below, indicate your level of agreement for each "fit" category.

This campus is a realistic...	Strongly Disagree	Disagree	Neither Agree nor Disagree	Agree	Strongly Agree
Academic Fit:	○	○	○	○	○
Diversity Fit:	○	○	○	○	○
Social Fit:	○	○	○	○	○
Financial Fit:	○	○	○	○	○
Athletic Fit:	○	○	○	○	○
Overall Fit:	○	○	○	○	○

• • • • • • • • • • • • •

Next steps for this school:

☐ Start Application   ☐ Submit Mid-Year Transcripts   ☐ Alumni Interview

☐ Thank You Note   ☐ Request More Information   ☐ Pay App Fee

☐ Finish Application   ☐ Submit FAFSA   ☐ Pay Deposit

☐ Other:

STATUS & PROGRESS

Use the status circles to track your progress for each application deliverable for this university. Once the deliverable is complete, write the completion date in the "100%" circle.

Name of College _____

| APPLICATION | ○ | ○ | ○ | ○ | ○ | ○ | ○ | ○ | ○ | ○ | ○ |
| | 10% | | | | 50% | | | | 100% | N/A |

| ESSAY | ○ | ○ | ○ | ○ | ○ | ○ | ○ | ○ | ○ | ○ | ○ |
| | 10% | | | | 50% | | | | 100% | N/A |

| TEST SCORE SUBMISSIONS | ○ | ○ | ○ | ○ | ○ | ○ | ○ | ○ | ○ | ○ | ○ |
| | 10% | | | | 50% | | | | 100% | N/A |

| TEACHER RECS | ○ | ○ | ○ | ○ | ○ | ○ | ○ | ○ | ○ | ○ | ○ |
| | 10% | | | | 50% | | | | 100% | N/A |

| COUNSELOR RECS | ○ | ○ | ○ | ○ | ○ | ○ | ○ | ○ | ○ | ○ | ○ |
| | 10% | | | | 50% | | | | 100% | N/A |

| SUPPLEMENT/ EXPRESSION PAGE | ○ | ○ | ○ | ○ | ○ | ○ | ○ | ○ | ○ | ○ | ○ |
| | 10% | | | | 50% | | | | 100% | N/A |

| FAFSA | ○ | ○ | ○ | ○ | ○ | ○ | ○ | ○ | ○ | ○ | ○ |
| | 10% | | | | 50% | | | | 100% | N/A |

| SCHOLARSHIP APP #1 | ○ | ○ | ○ | ○ | ○ | ○ | ○ | ○ | ○ | ○ | ○ |
| | 10% | | | | 50% | | | | 100% | N/A |

| SCHOLARSHIP APP #2 | ○ | ○ | ○ | ○ | ○ | ○ | ○ | ○ | ○ | ○ | ○ |
| | 10% | | | | 50% | | | | 100% | N/A |

| _____ | ○ | ○ | ○ | ○ | ○ | ○ | ○ | ○ | ○ | ○ | ○ |
| | 10% | | | | 50% | | | | 100% | N/A |

BIG IDEAS & RANDOM THOUGHTS

These are bullet pages. Use them as you wish - for notes, to-do lists, to sketch, draw or schedule tasks. Let your imagination drive you.

I'm Curious...

What do you hope to accomplish while in college? Come up with as many goals as you can.

BIG IDEA!
Send this description
to your guidance
counselor so s/he can
use it when writing
your letter of
recommendation.

NOTES

NOTES

RESOURCES

You've arrived at one of the most helpful places throughout your college search process. In the next few pages, you will find the following resources:

- Financial aid starting points
- Scholarship resources
- College ranking websites
- Sample text to use when communicating with campus personnel
- Commonly used key terms

HELPFUL WEBSITES

Financial Student Aid
FAFSA (Free Application for Federal Student Aid)
- https://studentaid.ed.gov/sa/fafsa

CSS Profile
- https://cssprofile.collegeboard.org/

Scholarships
- U.S. Government Federal Student Aid: http://bit.ly/FederalStudentAidScholarships
- Fastweb: www.fastweb.com
- Education USA: http://bit.ly/EdUSAFinAid
- College Board: http://bit.ly/CBAidSearch
- United Negro College Fund (UNCF): https://www.uncf.org/
- Hispanic School Fund (HSF): https://www.hsf.net/
- Scholarships A-Z: http://www.scholarshipsaz.org/scholarships/
- Asian & Pacific Islander American Scholarship Fund: https://apiascholars.org/
- American Indian Graduate Center: https://www.aigcs.org/scholarships-fellowships/
- Ask your counselor or advisor about local scholarship opportunities
- Check with churches, professional organizations, interest groups, affinity groups, etc.

College Rankings & Information
- U.S. News and World Report: https://www.usnews.com/education
- College Navigator: https://nces.ed.gov/collegenavigator/
- College Scorecard: https://collegescorecard.ed.gov/
- College Hunch: https://www.collegehunch.com/

Test Prep Resources
- Check your local library for additional books and guides
- ACT: Act.org
- SAT: collegereadiness.collegeboard.org/sat
- ACT Free Test Prep: http://bit.ly/ACTAcademyTestPrep
- SAT Free Test Prep: https://www.khanacademy.org/test-prep/sat

Virtual Campus Tour Resources
- SCOIR: https://www.scoir.com/
- You Visit: https://www.youvisit.com/collegesearch

Other Resources
- National College Access Network (NCAN): http://bit.ly/NCANforStudents

WRITING SAMPLES

Use the text below as a guide to send the following types of emails:

* Thank You Note
* Meeting Request with Professor, Dean or Coach
* Request to Visit a College Class

Thank You Note

Dear _____,

I wanted to thank you for _____. I appreciate the time you spent _____ (*verb + ing*) about _____ (*noun*). One thing that really stood out to me was _____. Now that we've [*spoken / met / etc.*], my plans are to _____. I will be sure to keep you updated along my journey. Thanks again for your time, and I hope to cross paths in the future.

Kindly,
[Your name here]
[Contact info] (phone, email, website, etc) (*Optional*)

Meeting Request with Professor, Dean or Coach

Greetings [Admission Counselor Name Here],

I am scheduled to visit [*campus or school name here*] on [*date*] and [*time*] and would like to see if I can meet with [*professor / dean / coach, etc. name here*] from the [*department / area / school / athletic team*]. I am very interested in [*name of program / sport / area of study / etc.*] and [*have questions about _____*] or [*would like to explore potential opportunities in _____*] with them.

Are you able to facilitate [or set up] a 15-minute meeting with them on my behalf?

Kindly,
[Your name here]
[Contact info] (phone, email, website, etc) (*Optional*)

Request to Visit a College Class

Greetings [Admission Counselor Name Here],

I am scheduled to visit [campus or school name here] on [*date*] and [*time*] and would like to sit in on a class during my visit. I am interested in visiting a [*department / area / school*] class if possible while I am on campus. Can you provide additional information about available classes, and alternatives if my desired classes aren't available?

Kindly,
[Your name here]
[Contact info] (phone, email, website, etc) (*Optional*)

KEY TERMS

ADA (Americans with Disabilities Act)
- The ADA Standards ensure access to the built environment for people with disabilities. They establish design requirements for the construction and alteration of facilities subject to the law.
  Source: https://www.access-board.gov/

COA (Cost of Attendance)
- The cost to attend the university.

CSS Profile
- A web-based financial aid form required mostly by private colleges. Processing fees are charged, so only colleges requiring the profile should receive it.

Early Action (non-binding)
- Students receive an early response from the college about their application, usually by the end of the calendar year (November or December).

Early Decision (binding)
- You commit to attend a school. When you apply and receive notice of admission early, you agree to attend that school and must withdraw all other applications. Generally, you can't change your mind once you've committed.

EFC (Expected Family Contribution)
- Expected Family Contribution. This is calculated upon submitting your FAFSA. It shows how much your family can afford to pay toward your college tuition for the year.

Gap
- Out-of-pocket amount after financial aid has been awarded. For example, if you owe $10,000 in tuition and fees for the year and receive $6,000 in financial aid, the remaining $4,000 is the out-of-pocket amount and is known as the gap.

Test Optional
- Also known as test flexible. An increasing number of universities de-emphasize the use of standardized tests by making admissions decisions -- without using ACT or SAT scores -- for all or many recent high school grads. For an up-to-date list of colleges and universities that are test optional, visit http://fairtest.org/university/optional

Verification
- The process a college uses to confirm that the data reported on your FAFSA is accurate.

Made in United States
North Haven, CT
03 February 2022